Executive Protection:
New Solutions
for a
New Era

by
Robert L. Oatman, CPP
600 Fairmount Avenue, Suite 101
Towson, MD 21286
phone (410) 494-1126
fax (410) 494-1163
www.rloatman.com

Executive Protection: New Solutions for a New Era

Copyright © 2006 Robert L. Oatman

Library of Congress
Cataloging in Publication Data
ISBN 1-56167-942-9

Library of Congress Card Catalog Number:
2006904744

First edition

Published by

Noble House

8019 Belair Road, Suite 10
Baltimore, Maryland 21236

Manufactured in the United States of America

Pursuing opportunity in the global marketplace puts corporate executives in contact with many risks. At home and abroad, businesspeople—especially those who stand as visible symbols of their companies—may be targets of calculating criminals, opportunists, philosophical adversaries, and even terrorists. Mr. Oatman understands that executives need to be able to operate safely and effectively wherever and whenever opportunity knocks. This book presents essential, low-key, and practical guidance for executives and their protectors based on Mr. Oatman's wide experience in analyzing risks and developing protection plans for corporate clients.

Christopher M. Connor
Chairman and CEO
The Sherwin-Williams Company

Throughout the United States, domestic terrorists have attacked government agencies, commercial businesses, and nonprofit organizations like ours, the Southern Poverty Law Center. In 1983, the Center's office was burned by Klansmen, and over the years several plots to bomb the Center and kill me have been thwarted. For a decade now, our executive protection specialists have been trained at Mr. Oatman's EP school. His practical, real-world approach to protective services places a premium on thorough planning and skillful execution to achieve "seamless" protection. This new book provides readers with many of the life-saving insights and up-to-date tools our EP specialists use every day.

Morris S. Dees
Founder and Chief Trial Counsel
Southern Poverty Law Center

As chief security officer for a *Fortune* 50 company, I pay close attention to the changing threats that top corporate executives face today. Dangers arise from many sources, old and new, known and unforeseen. The observations, techniques, and EP vision that Mr. Oatman's book provides will help EP specialists safeguard their protectees as they live and work in a fast-changing world. I urge readers to take advantage of the book's advice and prepare themselves for the unexpected.

Mark J. Cheviron

Corporate Vice President and Director of Security and Services
Archer Daniels Midland Company

Member, Executive Working Group
Overseas Security Advisory Council, U.S. Department of State

Member, Board of Directors
International Security Management Association

Executive Protection: New Solutions for a New Era serves as a vital resource for protection specialists and their protectees—especially for all those who live in, work in, or travel to countries with high rates of kidnapping, murder, and other crime. This timely book presents many practical tools and theoretical techniques, all geared toward strengthening an executive's ability to work successfully in a dangerous world.

Ricardo Torres Escotto, CPP, CPO

Chief Executive Officer, Grupo Corporativo de Proteccion Patrimonial
(Corporate Group of Assets Protection)

Chairman, Mexico Chapter, ASIS International

Bob Oatman's comprehensive approach, presented artfully in this new book, achieves two goals. It captures the multitude of details that a protection specialist must master: the schedules, logistics, equipment needs, and surprises that shape each day. It also helps readers visualize and grasp the big picture: the individual, local, national, and international currents and forces that constantly influence protectees' level of risk.

Edmund F. McDowell, Jr.
Special Agent in Charge, Uniformed Division and
Firearms Training Division, Retired
United States Secret Service

Dedication

This book is affectionately dedicated
to my wife, Janice, whose good
cheer, understanding, and support
have made all my work possible.

Acknowledgments

A book like this does not spring fully formed from the author's mind. Rather, it is the product of years of experience, months of painstaking research, and weeks of feedback from colleagues.

The origin of my expertise in executive protection lies in 20 years of service with the Baltimore County Police Department (BCPD), from which I retired as Major, Chief of Detectives, in 1989. That law enforcement experience provided insights into supervision, management, hostage negotiation, dignitary protection, and a host of other responsibilities that have enriched my understanding of, and ability to perform, executive protection. My BCPD roots run deep and wide, and they support my firm's protective and training efforts daily. For that I am grateful.

I also thank the FBI National Academy, a program for law enforcement leaders, for the training and networking it has provided. Likewise, training and networking I have gained from the United States Secret Service has been invaluable in the executive protection field.

ASIS International, formerly the American Society for Industrial Security, has been an invaluable resource and partner. I have taught and learned from untold numbers of security professionals through my opportunities to present at the ASIS Annual Seminar & Exhibits, which draws a worldwide following, for more than a decade. The same is true of my eight years of teaching a two-day EP program for ASIS International around the country. I offer special thanks to Susan Melnicove, Director of Education, and Ursula Uszynski, Senior Educational Programs Manager. My contacts at ASIS also encouraged me to study for and obtain the ASIS Certified Protection Professional designation.

Thanks also go out to the protection professionals who encouraged me to establish the Oatman School of Executive Protection, now in its 12th year. They include Michael Bruggeman of General Motors Corporation, Mark Cheviron of Archer Daniels Midland Company, Thomas Brinkman of the Southern Poverty Law Center, Jim Esposito of the New York Stock Exchange, Master Sergeant Richard Cannon of the U.S. Southern Command, John Lugiano, and many others, who all have my sincere appreciation.

My friend and colleague Richard Heaps has provided good counsel and a steady hand in managing the daily operations of R. L. Oatman & Associates since the beginning.

I thank the expert faculty of our EP school, who have dedicated their time, knowledge, experience, and hard work toward making the program innovative, creative, and successful. They have helped train EP specialists from around the world, and they have become my good friends in the process.

With much appreciation, I acknowledge the guidance of a valuable mentor, Theodore Shackley, who passed away in 2002. He is sorely missed, but his influence continues.

I am grateful to my daughter and son, who even as adults have woven their lives together with mine and who contribute much to the success of my endeavors.

Fond appreciation goes to Peter Ohlhausen, a colleague and friend who provided major support in the creation of this book. As a writer and researcher in criminal justice and security—and, significantly, an experienced member of the R. L. Oatman & Associates consulting team—he turned his knowledge and skills toward the arduous task of clearly expressing my vision of executive protection.

Robert L. Oatman
May 2006

Foreword

Our country and its citizens face many dangers today, both at home and abroad. International terrorists and other criminals target innocent civilians in many settings: workplaces, schools, transportation facilities, and more. The right response, however, is not fear or paralysis but the hard work of learning about the threats and taking preventive actions. I believe good intelligence is the best defense against terrorism.

The author of this book, Robert Oatman, through his work in the field of executive protection, safeguards people who, because of their occupations or success in business, may be especially targeted by adversaries, whether terrorists or other criminals.

This book spells out, in theoretical and practical terms, the hazards that face "principals" or those individuals who most need personal protection. It emphasizes the ways in which the threat has changed since the terrorist attacks of September 11, 2001. Various chapters clarify the importance of protecting these principals, many of whom are valuable keystones of our nation's economic strength; the practicality and benefits of intelligence-based, behind-the-scenes protection services; the right relation between security technology and risk avoidance; the crucial importance of training for those who provide personal protection; and the balance between protection and freedom.

Our country's efforts to boost port security have shown that it is vital to protect assets without disabling them. Too much security can be almost as harmful as too little. Mr. Oatman's book rightly makes the point that the best protection measures actually improve an industry's or an individual's ability to function, rather than overly restricting the protected resource and preventing it from doing its job. And the book does more than make that point: it tells the reader how to safeguard at-risk executives without restricting their ability to perform the work they do best.

In a sense, all who work to protect our nation and its citizens are part of the same team. The military uses different methods than the police, who use different methods than private protection specialists. Intelligence-gathering capabilities are different at the federal level than on the personal level. But despite those differences, the goal is the same: protecting our nation, its citizens, and our priceless freedoms.

Hon. C. A. "Dutch" Ruppersberger
U.S. House of Representatives

Contents

Introduction 1

1. A Different World 7

2. Practical Value of Executive Protection 11
   Asset Protection 12
   Asset Optimization 14
   Return on Investment 15
   Guiding Rules 16
   Case Studies 17

3. Risk Assessment 25
   General Risk Assessment Methodologies 28
   Threat Tracking 34
   Elements of EP Risk Assessment 36
   Linking It All Together 54

4. Means of Attack and Lessons Learned 57
   The Bomb 58
   The Gun 66
   Kidnapping 70
   Other Attacks 80

5. Countersurveillance 83
   What, Why, and When 83
   Surveillance by Adversaries 85
   Countersurveillance Methods 88
   Antisurveillance 93

6. It's Not About the Gun 101
   Limitations 103
   Permits 104
   Training 108
   Detecting Armed Adversaries 109
   Travel Considerations 111
   Step-Down Weapons 112

7. Technology in Protective Operations 115
   Communication 117

Navigation 119
Tracking 119
Photography 120
Information Gathering 120
Alarm Systems 127
Emergency Response 127

8. Know Before You Go **131**
Sample Trip 133
Pre-Advance 135
Airport Advance 139
Ground Transportation Advance 140
Route Advance 141
Lodging Advance 142

9. Local Travel **145**
The Driver 148
The Route 153
The Vehicle 154

10. Long-Distance Travel **161**
General EP Travel Considerations 161
Commercial Air Travel 172
Private Flight Operations 177

11. Training and Certification **193**
General Importance of Training 193
Training Schools 194
Certifications 201

12. Managing and Directing an EP Detail **205**
Risk Assessment 207
Program Development 208

Appendix **219**
A. Mail Screening Tips 221
B. Bomb Threat Card 223
C. Checklists for Advance Work 225

Index **241**

Introduction

Everyone faces certain hazards in life, but some people are targeted more than others. Top corporate executives and wealthy or famous families increasingly turn to executive protection (EP) specialists for help in reducing the dangers that their positions in life attract. A maturing, increasingly professional specialty, EP is now a necessity for many.

This book carries forward the theme of the author's previous volume, *The Art of Executive Protection*, first published in 1997 and now in its fifth printing. That book presents the timeless fundamentals of executive protection and continues to be an essential reference.

The present volume, *Executive Protection: New Solutions for a New Era*, builds on the first book, not attempting to cover all facets of EP but instead presenting a fresh look at EP topics that have changed the most since the September 11, 2001, terror attacks that shook the United States. Those terrible events brought security into the spotlight like never before. Interest in executive protection—even among people who had never previously considered it—rose to new heights.

This book expands on the basic and advanced concepts of executive protection, adapting them to the post-9/11 era and updating them to reflect developments in global trade, international travel, corporate responsibility, and advanced technologies.

Written for those who provide protection and those who require it, the book begins with an examination of the world's current threat trends. It then discusses the practical value of EP in a corporate environment and describes the techniques of the all-important risk assessment, on which any intelligent protection program must be based. Additional chapters describe real attacks against executives by various means, countersurveillance, the roles of firearms and technology in EP, local and long-distance travel, training and management of EP staff, and other vital topics. (As a bonus, the book provides on-line access to advance checklists at www.rloatman.com.) The book emphasizes protective measures appropriate to a private-sector protective effort, with typical private-sector resources and capabilities, rather than a public-sector protective effort with the full force of a government behind it. In other words, the book describes how to protect a principal without being able to stop traffic for a security convoy or call in military-grade assistance. It focuses primarily on protection of corporate executives but also addresses protection of wealthy private families and of government officials who do not have a full protective detail.

The goal of EP—and of this book—is to safeguard those who face above-average personal risk due to their high positions in business or government or the special characteristics of their family profile.

Through long, varied experience, the author has developed three guiding rules that embody the philosophy of executive protection:

1. Be systemic, not symptomatic.
2. Be proactive, not reactive.
3. Choose flight, not a fight.

Those rules, which should guide an EP specialist's decision-making in all aspects of EP, are explained in Chapter 3: Risk Assessment.

What makes executive protection so important? Many executives consider it unlikely that harm will come to them. They may be comfortable with risk-taking, and they may have the impression that attacks against executives are rare. However, such attacks occur more often than is commonly thought, and the outcomes can be disastrous for both the victims and their organizations. The following account describes the kidnapping of a successful businessman.

Lampert Case

The January 10, 2003, kidnapping of hedge-fund executive Edward Lampert, age 40, from his Greenwich office is a highly significant threat indicator for U.S. business executives. Potential protectees may emphasize that Mr. Lampert survived the kidnapping, but his survival was a close call, as the kidnappers were armed and had military training. Many aspects of the case should serve as a flashing red warning light to executives who think they would never be kidnapped.

The details are as follows: Mr. Lampert was grabbed from the parking garage of his investment-company headquarters in Connecticut by several men, who held him at a hotel for two days. The kidnappers wielded a shotgun and kept Mr. Lampert blindfolded and handcuffed in a bathtub.

About 30 hours after his abduction, he was freed unharmed, even though the demand for a $5 million ransom was not met. When police found the kidnappers in their hotel room, they found a mask, a shotgun, and seven rounds of ammunition.

Two of the three kidnappers were fresh from prison after serving stretches for drug dealing, according to Connecticut officials. Mr. Lampert was a known billionaire, the second-richest person in Connecticut, and was listed on the *Forbes* 400 list of richest Americans. As *USA Today* noted, "That made him the target of Renaldo Rose, 23, a former Marine who **scoured the Internet for a rich person to kidnap** [emphasis added]."[1] Rose also followed Mr. Lampert for several weeks, *Greenwich Time* reported.

Another noteworthy aspect of the case is that the kidnap ringleader was planning to use the stolen brown uniform of a UPS driver to gain entry to Mr. Lampert's office. There has also been a claim that the kidnappers were hired to kill Mr. Lampert because of his association with certain business deals.

Elements of concern include the following:

- Mr. Lampert was a working businessman, not a readily recognizable rock star, heir to a well-known fortune, or especially controversial figure.
- Mr. Lampert lived and worked in extremely safe jurisdictions.
- The kidnappers targeted him based on universally available information from the Internet.
- The kidnappers used low-tech, inexpensive means to carry out the kidnapping: a young person on a bicycle to conduct surveillance at the office parking site, a beaten-up van in which to carry the victim away, an inexpensive motel room for concealing the victim, and a simple shotgun.

A kidnapping like that of Mr. Lampert is dangerous, distressing, and disruptive enough, but even greater risk is faced by executives who live or travel outside the United States, who are easily recognized, or who represent a controversial organization, industry, or country. This book presents many case studies of attacks

---

[1] David Lieberman, "Lampert's potent force in investing branches into retailing," *USA Today*, November 22, 2004.

against executives, some with dire endings. It is important to take those illustrations and the world's risks seriously—not so seriously as to become paralyzed with fear or resignation, but seriously enough to take action to reduce the threats. This book is written to guide executive protection specialists and those they protect in their efforts to preserve executive safety and productivity.

1.
A Different World

The United States is at war now, facing down terrorists around the globe. For many executives, this is a high-risk era. It is also a time for EP specialists to carry out the fundamentals of executive protection while opening their minds to additional protective techniques against a wider range of threats.

Terrorism is not the primary threat that corporate executives and wealthy persons face today. However, terrorism has changed the canvas on which EP specialists work, and it has heightened executives' interest in security. Public responses to terrorism—military actions and stricter security around public buildings and transport centers—may deflect the attention of terrorists and other criminals away from such hard targets toward softer, nongovernmental targets. The effects of terrorism even spread to EP logistical planning. For example, when the Twin Towers of the World Trade Center fell on September 11, 2001, EP specialists throughout New York worked hurriedly to evacuate their protectees from the city. Some of those EP specialists were better prepared than others. As a result of that experience, it has become common practice to develop evacuation plans even from U.S. cities—a measure that earlier was undertaken mainly for overseas travel.

Likewise, the July 7, 2005, London bombings led some to ask whether the time had come to get used to terrorist attacks. The answer, of course, is yes and no. Clearly, terror attacks seem to be targeting urban business areas in which executives might be expected to spend time. Thus, there is legitimate cause to conclude that the risk of encountering a terrorist attack may be growing, and one should get used to the idea of an attack—in the specific sense of getting ready for an attack. If, on the other hand, getting used to it means developing a sense of complacency, then naturally one should not get used to the threat.

Clearly, the new patterns of terrorism are influencing the demand for EP service and the way in which that service is provided. To help protectees and EP specialists better understand those patterns, this chapter takes a brief look at the geopolitical backdrop of contemporary terrorism.

Before September 11, 2001, any American businessperson or government figure could travel the world in reasonable confidence that he or she knew how to assess the terrorist threat. But changes were already developing. First, state-supported terrorism was in decline. Second, forced to become more self-reliant, and motivated more by religion or ideology than politics, terrorists regrouped into loose networks of small cells, abandoning the hierarchical structure of groups like the Japanese Red Army or the Red Army Fraction of Germany. The latter case is particularly instructive. The Red Army Fraction started operating in May 1970. Over its 18-year life it carried out a series of bombings and kidnappings, and it assassinated more than 50 people, including high-ranking German politicians, business executives, and American military personnel. Then, on April 20, 1998, the group announced that it had formally disbanded, being "stuck in a dead end." One reason the group disbanded was that after 1990 East Germany, which had previously supported the group, no longer existed, and the Red Army Fraction could no longer function effectively.

A third change in the character of terrorism was that bombs became ever more clearly the weapon of choice.

The September 11 attacks were the culmination of those trends. America is now at war with terrorism, and its strategy is designed for fighting and wining a protracted war over an enemy—international terrorism—that is difficult to define. The enemy is not a state, and it is difficult to find where its members train, how they obtain equipment and funds, and where they take shelter before deploying for combat. Moreover, there are no clearly defined battlefields. The U.S. strategy, therefore, is significantly different from what it was in the past. In a constantly changing mix, it combines covert operations, military strikes, diplomacy, financial sanctions, police work, and psychological warfare.

In short, the U.S. has been pushed into a new kind of conflict with new battlefields. The world is indeed different from what it was before September 11, 2001.

This change affects everyone. In the past, corporations tended to follow the lead of the U.S. State Department in deciding whether to operate in high-threat foreign environments. However, the State Department is not infallible. Moreover, it is influenced—as it should be—by broader national policy interests than the interests that shape corporate destinies. Thus, it is not prudent for corporations to follow to the letter State Department decisions on risk and security threats.

In February 1998, a religious decree called a *fatwa* was issued by a coalition of Islamic groups in London, advocating attacks on

American civilians until U.S. forces retreated from Saudi Arabia. The group claimed the *fatwa* had been drafted by Muslim religious authorities in Lebanon, Jordan, and Palestine. At the same time, a group headed by Osama bin Laden issued a statement in Afghanistan which said, "The ruling to kill the Americans and their allies, both civilians and military, is an individual duty for every Muslim who can do it, no matter where he lives. We must liberate the holy mosque in Mecca from their grip." The CIA has pointed out that these were the first religious rulings explicitly justifying attacks on American citizens anywhere in the world.

The September 11 attacks were carried out by 19 men from Saudi Arabia, Lebanon, Jordan, and Egypt. They were well-educated, clever, and sufficiently motivated to enter the United States and blend into ordinary suburban lives. Then they gained just enough training as pilots to take control of passenger jets in mid-air and use them to hit preselected targets.

They were able to play dual roles, living secretly and, at the same time, out in the open. From an EP standpoint, that is an accomplishment that merits study. They used fundamental techniques of spy or criminal tradecraft, such as prepaid cellular telephones or discreet direct meetings among themselves. They avoided strangers. In addition, they were innovative, performing Internet searches at public libraries to avoid being traced. In short, their tradecraft was low-tech but effective. Moreover, the entire operation appears to have cost its sponsors not much more than $500,000.

The story of September 11 teaches, among other lessons, that a focused adversary can cause terrible damage with modest resources. It also teaches that attacks can come from unexpected directions. In this era of elevated risk—from a great variety of sources—it is all the more important to do the job of executive protection right.

2.
Practical Value of Executive Protection

In the field of executive protection, misconceptions abound. Persons unfamiliar with EP may feel the service is a showy corporate luxury, or a stifling burden, or a precaution needed only by the famous. All those perceptions are mistaken. Executive protection is a practical, helpful service, scaled to individual risks and needs, that helps create a safe environment in which business executives and their companies can flourish.

EP serves two clear corporate functions: asset protection (keeping the executive and corporate reputation safe from harm) and asset optimization (boosting productivity by improving convenience and freeing the executive from some major tasks and concerns of personal security). The activities that comprise executive protection serve both of those functions simultaneously and inseparably. This chapter examines both asset protection and asset optimization, shows how to analyze the return on investment (ROI) in executive protection, and then presents several case studies of EP programs.

Asset Protection

A company's top executives are among its greatest assets. The incapacitation or loss of those executives would clearly diminish the organization's ability to carry out its mission. Companies are already in the habit of protecting their physical and information assets. EP takes that habit a logical step further and protects certain of the company's human assets. The decision on whether and how vigorously to protect those assets is based on a detailed risk assessment (explained more fully in Chapter 3).

What, exactly, could happen to an executive? Is his or her life really so risky? The risk level is determined in the risk assessment, but the types of harm that regularly occur to business executives include kidnapping, workplace violence, attacks by protesters (dangerous, humiliating, or both), terror attacks (against overseas American interests, such as hotels), street crime, and accidental injury (especially related to travel: car crashes, hotel fires, etc.).

Some corporate assets—office buildings, factories, retail stores—stay in one place. For those assets, a security effort may also be able to stay in one place. By contrast, an executive moves around. Whether the executive is attacked in the office, while driving to work, during a trip, or back at his or her home, the result is much the same: the organization loses a valuable asset. For that reason, any EP effort must take into account the risks that the executive faces at all hours of the day, not just 9 to 5. The risk assessment may show that the executive does not need to be accompanied by EP staff outside of work hours but does require a high-quality security alarm system at home, possibly even a safe room[2] in the house, and perhaps some training in protective driving.

Many executives spend most of their time in safe places (such as their office, home, or club). However, they may venture into higher-crime areas when they dine out, attend a concert, or drive through a dangerous neighborhood on their way to someplace else. Executive protection has to take a comprehensive view. It would do little good to protect the executive at the office, only to allow him or her to be attacked in the evening. Again, the solution may or may not be to establish personal protection during off-hours. At the risk level that many executives face, an appropriate protective response might be as simple as asking the principal or an executive assistant to inform the EP specialist of the principal's outing plans a little in advance so the EP specialist can offer advice as to the safest ways in and out of the location or event. The level of risk may be higher or lower at different locations and different times of day, but some risk is always present, and the EP specialist has a responsibility to minimize that risk.

A corporation has good reason to protect its executives. The case of Italian fashion designer Gianni Versace illustrates what can happen when the top executive of a large corporation is lost. After Mr. Versace was murdered in Miami Beach in 1997, news reports focused on the loss to the fashion world, and celebrities gathered

---

[2] A safe room is a space in which a principal can wait securely for a short time while police or security staff rush to the scene. When the risk assessment shows a need for a safe room, it is possible to refit a closet, restroom, or other small space (at home or at work) for that purpose. The room should be outfitted with a strong, solid, locking door to protect the occupant. In addition, the room should be stocked with two trickle-charged flashlights with a supply of batteries for backup, a small fire extinguisher, an advanced first aid kit, drinking water, a hard-line telephone (normal wired phone), and a cellular phone (no service subscription needed; if battery is charged, the phone will still dial 911).

to mourn him. But the death of the famous designer had other implications as well. His corporation, a major, international business that was about to go public, suffered an expensive blow.

At the time of Mr. Versace's death, the company had been preparing itself for an initial public offering. "I want [the company] to be perfect when we go to the market," he told *Business Week* shortly before his death. Valuing the business at up to $1.5 billion, the stock offering was shaping up as one of Europe's hottest for 1998. Upon Mr. Versace's death, the IPO was suspended. As of 2006, the company, though still in business, had not recovered sufficiently to renew its plans to go public.

From an EP standpoint, what happened? A vital asset of the corporation was left unprotected and thus was lost.

Asset Optimization

Economist John Maynard Keynes wrote that many of people's decisions to do something positive "can only be taken as the result of animal spirits—and not as the outcome of a weighted average of quantitative benefits multiplied by quantitative probabilities." He further observed, "If the animal spirits are dimmed and the spontaneous optimism falters…enterprise will fade and die."

Keynes meant that objective calculations are not the only driver of business activity—there must be an entrepreneurial spark as well. The "animal spirits" inspire businesspeople to take risks, to explore, to act. In the period immediately following September 11, 2001, there were signs that the animal spirits had grown meek in some quarters. Business travel declined, conference attendance was down, and uncertainty about the future was high.

This is where EP plays an important role. Executives do indeed face special dangers at present, but the threats are not all equally relevant to every company decision-maker. EP can help executives decide which dangers are serious and which are less so for their own unique situations. EP can also reduce those dangers, enabling executives to concentrate on business and giving them the necessary confidence to travel in search of opportunities. In a high-risk era, EP can free executives to do the work they do best.

Return on Investment

Executive protection, like other organizational programs, can be examined from a return on investment (ROI) standpoint. An EP program provides both tangible and intangible returns. Tangible returns include increased productivity through executives' ability to work undistracted by threats, avoidance of physical damage to the facility, avoidance of downtime, and avoidance of lawsuits for failure to provide a safe workplace. Intangible benefits include reduction of stress and improvement of the organization's image. Both the tangible and intangible benefits, or returns, can affect the success of the organization's mission. A good EP program costs less than the benefits it produces and the damage it prevents. Moreover, increased security designed to protect the principals will end up also protecting everyone who works with them.

Even an attack that causes no serious injury can bring unflattering attention to an organization and raise questions about its competence and preparedness. Such attention and questions can affect an organization's reputation in the public eye, among clients, and, perhaps, on Wall Street.

The following is a concrete, quantitative example of the economic value of executive protection: [3]

> Showing how an executive protection team can maximize the use of an executive's time drives home the security function's return on investment (ROI). One Japanese financial institution uses protective services for just this reason. Besides protecting its rainmakers, this company has found that, on average, it saves the executive 2.5 hours per day because of the protection agent's ability to speed his charge through check-

---

[3] Christopher J. Simovich, "To Serve and Protect," *Security Management*, October 2004, p. 80.

points and immigration stops…. [T]his translates into a minimum $3,400 in savings per day per executive.

Guiding Rules

Three guiding rules may help EP specialists organize their thinking and their protective efforts. The rules may also help potential protectees understand that executive protection is a thoughtful, careful effort that avoids inconvenience and confrontation.

1. Be systemic, not symptomatic.
2. Be proactive, not reactive.
3. Choose flight, not a fight.

Be Systemic, Not Symptomatic

This rule urges EP specialists to understand the complete picture of risks and protective measures, address all relevant elements of protective operations, avoid the urge to plug small holes without solving underlying problems, and apply simple, sometimes basic measures consistently across many domains. The graphic at right illustrates the connectedness of the various realms of vulnerability.

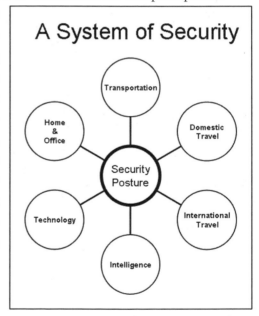

A System of Security

Transportation

Home & Office

Domestic Travel

Security Posture

Technology

International Travel

Intelligence

Be Proactive, Not Reactive

This rule encourages EP specialists to look forward and outward. That means conducting threat assessments, weighing and managing risks, appropriately applying resources, and performing countersurveillance. The opposite approach—event-driven response—

can result in excessive security measures, over-engineering, inflated deployment of security personnel, and unnecessary inconvenience to the protectee.

Choose Flight, Not a Fight

The primary purpose of EP is not to capture or kill attackers but to protect the executive. Experience shows that, in this context, escaping from an attack leads to better outcomes than standing one's ground and fighting back. Therefore, the EP specialist should develop plans that emphasize getting the protectee away from danger or else finding cover. Preparing for a safe escape requires detailed advance preparation, including site surveys and training for a near-automatic execution of the exit strategy.

Case Studies

Over the past several years, the author's firm has helped many organizations develop or strengthen their EP programs. In all cases, the companies wanted their executives to be safe, to feel safe, and to be able to focus on their work instead of the world's dangers. The following cases show how four organizations at very different stages of security development boosted their executive protection operations during the past several years. The appropriate EP response to current threats is also discussed.

High-Stress Work Environment

The wealthy president of a financial services company knew she needed some level of personal security measures. Her home had a high-end security system, complete with extensive perimeter protection and patrols. Her office featured CCTV, basic access control measures, and an attentive receptionist. However, her staff remarked on major gaps in her security. For example, the executive often drove herself to work and routinely drove her own car outside working hours.

At the office, workplace violence was a concern because of the high stress level there. (The principal worked in a roomful of frantic traders.) The CCTV images at the office were not closely monitored.

Another concern was that the garage under the executive's office building was readily accessible to passersby. Further, her young children were spread out at several schools, where they ran the risk of being kidnapped because of their mother's wealth.

To address those issues, the company commissioned a risk assessment, which determined that the principal's home was a particularly attractive target in its neighborhood and that the executive's personal profile had recently increased substantially because of media coverage of her activities. It also found that businesses like hers had recently experienced significant workplace violence from employees and clients, and that her children faced increasing risk as they grew older and participated in more activities outside the home.

In response, the company established a new EP manager position so that one person would be focused on addressing those issues for the executive. It also assigned a trained EP driver to the principal and her family.

In addition, the company took steps to improve general security in the workplace. For example, employees were required to wear ID badges so that executive assistants (a second line of defense after the building's main lobby reception desk) could determine whom to admit into the company's executive suite. In addition, the badges doubled as access cards (with proximity technology) and served as convenient keys so that more areas of the office, such as the trading room in which the executive worked, could be kept locked even during the day.

The company built a special garage with a private entrance to the building so the principal could park in a highly secure location and reach her office without any exposure to the public. Further, CCTV coverage of the executive's garage area and office entrance was routed to the reception desk. That arrangement gave the receptionist the ability to watch for suspicious persons in those areas.

Only a few months after those measures were implemented, an executive in the same town and same line of work was kidnapped for ransom. Although one can never know for certain, perhaps the executive with the improved EP program was not targeted because of the improved protection.

Conspicuous Targets

In another case, a wealthy married couple worked full-time operating their charitable foundation. Their home had extensive physical security measures and armed, roving patrols managed by a contract service. However, their office was protected by only a basic electronic security system, and the two principals routinely drove themselves around town.

They were well known and easily recognized in their medium-sized city, which suffered a surprisingly high crime rate. In addition, their plans called for extensive travel on their private aircraft to many dangerous regions around the world.

The principals and their staff recognized that a risk assessment might be wise, given the known gaps in security and their planned travel to high-risk locales. The assessment discovered that the principals' wealth was described at many Web sites and that their address and photos were available on-line.

The assessment also revealed that their current home stood out as a desirable target and had been the target of numerous suspicious visits, calls, and letters. The couple also had a new home in the planning stages at the time, and the assessment noted that the new residence, when completed, would stand out even more.

The office could be penetrated more easily than expected and had been previously burgled by an insider. In addition, the couple's private aircraft was so grand that, at any airport, it would in effect announce that a desirable target had just arrived.

19

Further, the principals routinely drove themselves through dangerous neighborhoods and parked in poorly lit downtown garages unaccompanied by security staff. Because they were well known, they were often approached by strangers when out in public.

Several preventive measures were put in place to address these vulnerabilities. First, the principals purchased low-profile protected vehicles[4] and took training in security driving techniques. They also established a practice of call-ahead communication to let security staff know their whereabouts and destinations at all times.

At the office, lighting and access control were improved. Safe rooms were added to both the home and the office. For the new home, a security engineer was engaged to make security suggestions while the project was still in the architectural design phase.

In addition, the principals hired a dedicated EP manager to manage security at home, at work, for local transit, and for out-of-town travel. Before major trips, the EP manager now conducts travel advances to plan evacuation strategies, arrange emergency medical care, establish liaisons with local law enforcement, assess on-the-ground threats, and coordinate protection efforts with local security providers who are knowledgeable about conditions at the site. The manager also usually meets the principals in their destination city with all arrangements confirmed and accompanies them on the flight home.

Personalized Protection

A large energy company headquartered in a high-crime city had a well-developed corporate security program, but it had no separate

---

[4] A protected vehicle, sometimes known an armored vehicle or armored car, has various security features that protect the occupants from a range of threats. Protected vehicles are discussed in detail in Chapter 8: Local Travel. The key point here is that many protected vehicles are indistinguishable from other vehicles and do not attract attention.

EP division. The CEO's rising public profile led security staff to request an in-depth risk assessment. That assessment found that while some of the top-echelon staff were in fairly little danger, others faced a high degree of risk.

As a result of the study, the company opted to develop a dedicated EP division and substantially increase certain elements of executive security. For example, the company developed stricter visitor sign-in procedures on the executive floor, purchased automated external defibrillators, arranged escorts to accompany the executives to the garage after dark, added a portable x-ray machine to the executive suite mailroom, and created safe rooms to which executives could flee in the event of an attack.

For local transportation, the company provided the executives' drivers with additional training in defensive driving and with basic training in executive protection. For commercial air travel, the company added security features to the in-house travel planner's computer to limit unauthorized access to executive travel plans.

The company also contractually required limousine services to conduct background checks on any drivers who would drive the principals in destination cities, provided the principals with detailed emergency contact cards, and briefed the principals on safe travel practices. For travel to high-risk locations or by the highest-risk principals, the company began to perform on-site advance visits and to arrange local security assistance at the destination city.

The new EP program established a 24-hour command, control, and communications center, and an EP manager was hired to run the program. For the highest-risk executives, the company opted to make full-time executive protection available, including transportation in protected vehicles. In addition, safe rooms were constructed at those executives' homes.

At this particular company, not all executives faced the same risk level. Some executives represented controversial aspects of the company, while others operated behind the scenes. Tailoring security measures to each executive's risk level enabled the lower-risk executives to feel free to perform their work and move about safely, and it protected the higher-risk executives sufficiently, giving them the confidence they needed to perform their duties. Once all of the company's executives were given the right level of protection, they were able to focus more on running the business and less on keeping themselves safe.

Meeting Evolving Threats

One of the largest manufacturing concerns in the world had a well-developed, elaborate EP program—one of the best the author has ever seen. After the September 11 attacks, however, the company decided to reevaluate the risk faced by its top tier of executives to determine whether they were receiving adequate security, given the changed threat profile.

The risk assessment determined that the company and its executives were more vulnerable to domestic terrorist groups (such as the Earth Liberation Front and the Animal Liberation Front) than previously thought. The assessment also revealed that the executives were not well protected during nonworking hours and on personal travel, that a significant amount of personal information about the executives was available on the Web, and that the company vehicles in which the executives were driven were not always kept in secure garages overnight.

In response to those findings, the company beefed up its threat-tracking system, increased EP coverage of executives during nonworking hours (such as during personal outings to high-crime areas of the city's downtown), reduced the amount of personal information about the executives on the corporate Web site, and arranged for secure parking of executive transport vehicles.

As a result, the executives were better protected, their families and staff felt more confident about the executives' safety, and the executives could better concentrate on their work.

Many companies are finding this the right moment to establish an EP program or to expand their existing EP operations. In so doing, they are creating an environment in which executives can best develop their animal spirits and help their companies get the lion's share of the available business opportunities.

3.
Risk Assessment

Risk assessment is a key, foundational step that distinguishes professional EP specialists from shoot-from-the-hip amateurs. A risk assessment analyzes what could happen to a protectee, how likely that threat is, how serious the outcome of an attack would be, and where the weak links in protection are. A risk assessment identifies potential dangers in an individual's living and working environments, in travel between those locations, and in personal activities. Not all persons living and working in a given location require the same degree of protection. Protection recommendations must be based on an assessment of the threats likely to be directed at the particular individual. The risk assessment enables security professionals to establish protection measures appropriate to the threat and to prioritize efforts so that security resources are applied in the most efficient manner.

Many large corporations, and many corporate executives, are at risk of attack from various adversaries. Individuals and groups may have personal grievances against the corporation or its executives, or they may hold objections over such issues as environmental practices, labor practices, national affiliation, use of animals in testing, role in the global marketplace, or involvement in controversial biomedical issues. Certainly, some corporations are more controversial than others, and some executives attract more animosity than others.

Moreover, for various adversaries, some targets have a greater public shock value than others. A recent article in *Time*[5] contained this quotation: "Killing one educated person is as effective as killing dozens of ordinary people." The statement was attributed to "an Afghan tribal elder, warning of the dangers of the Taliban—who last week beheaded a high school teacher—and its efforts to undermine trust in the government." In much the same way, attacks against top corporate executives hold a more powerful symbolism than attacks against some other targets.

At this moment in history, defense contractors may be at special risk. An article titled "Analysis: U.S. Defense Contractors: Are They a Potential Target?"[6] observes:

> Defense contractors provide an integral element to our economy and national security infrastructure.... [A]n attack on a defense contractor could prove to be very detrimental. Moreover, methodically planned concurrent attacks on multiple contractor facilities could prove disastrous.... Scientists, engineers and production crews would be in complete fear, crippling their ability to work. These individuals provide all aspects of material to the government. They provide support of innovative technologies, software, fighter jets, ships, tanks, radar equipment and especially precision guided missiles. To put it bluntly, the United States and its allies are totally dependent upon contractors to fulfill their operational needs.
>
> Production could be impaired or even halted depending on the nature or scope of the attack. A halt on production would cause great damage to the U.S. especially with the current

---

[5] "Notebook," *Time*, January 16, 2006.
[6] Author: Jesse Robert. Available at www.homelandsecurity.com.

demand for military hardware and technology in anticipation of conflicts overseas. Terrorist attacks could literally delay a buildup of weapons, and impair our ability to fight wars on multiple fronts....

Defense contractors are prepared for spies, industrial espionage, theft of trade secrets, proprietary processes and technology, natural disasters and perhaps even large public demonstrations.... However,...terrorism remains a very real threat to defense contractors, as they are seen from many people's perspective as the ones who enable our government to militarily dominate....

Defense contractors, although private sector, need to have the same protection and awareness as military bases and federal buildings.

Even when the risk of an incident is low, the cost and other impacts if an attack should occur may be enormous and therefore well worth preventing. Serious harm to an executive or his family members, interruption of business, and loss of employee and public confidence in the company are among the likely outcomes of a successful attack against a principal.

In the security field, the terms *threat assessment, risk assessment,* and *vulnerability assessment* are often used interchangeably—sometimes because of confusion regarding the terms, and sometimes because the type of assessment being conducted combines elements of all three types. In any case, it is useful to understand the distinction between the types. *Security Management* magazine, published by ASIS International,[7] published one rubric for differentiating the varieties of assessments:[8]

A threat assessment looks at what events could occur in a given environment. The risk assessment examines how likely they would be to occur in that environment and how much damage they would cause. The vulnerability assessment identifies weaknesses and examines how well existing countermeasures reduce the risk.

---

[7] Formerly called the American Society for Industrial Security International.

[8] "A Finer Point," *Security Management,* January 2005, p. 14.

In executive protection, the risk assessment generally combines elements of threat assessment and risk assessment, as defined above. In addition, threat assessment in EP tends to examine not just potential threats but also actual threats that have been made. In sum, it is not practical to be completely dogmatic in the use of the terms.

This chapter takes a look at the following:

- general risk assessment methodologies
- threat tracking
- elements of EP risk assessment

General Risk Assessment Methodologies

Various methods can be used to conduct threat and risk assessments. For example, the U.S. Department of Homeland Security (DHS) has created a report (the *Vulnerability Assessment Methodologies Report*[9]) that presents several means of conducting threat and risk assessments in support of effective security plans. The DHS report expresses risk as an equation:

$$Risk = Consequences \times Likelihood$$

Likelihood of occurrence is further defined as *threat* (any indication, circumstance, or event with the potential to cause loss or damage to an asset, taking into account the intention and capability of an adversary) times *vulnerability* (a weakness that can be exploited by an adversary to gain access to an asset, including building characteristics, security practices, personal behaviors, etc.).

Sandia National Laboratories, too, has developed risk assessment methodologies for various physical security applications and industries. Those risk assessments, though well known, are espe-

---

[9] U.S. Department of Homeland Security, *Vulnerability Assessment Methodologies Report* (Washington: 2003), available at www.ojp.usdoj.gov/odp/docs/vamreport.pdf.

cially complex and not oriented toward personal protection.

The risk assessment guideline produced by ASIS International[10] provides general recommendations for examining the universe of risk. Because it is a general guideline and not specifically designed for executive protection, it cannot be used directly for EP applications. However, it provides a useful service by helping readers understand the general steps in risk assessment and examine the broad range of risks and other considerations.

The following steps come from the ASIS International *General Security Risk Assessment Guideline*:

> 1. **Understand the organization and identify the people and assets at risk.** *Assets* include people, all types of property, core business, networks, and information. *People* include employees, tenants, guests, vendors, visitors, and others directly or indirectly connected or involved with an enterprise. *Property* includes tangible assets such as cash and other valuables and intangible assets such as intellectual property and causes of action. *Core business* includes the primary business or endeavor of an enterprise, including its reputation and goodwill. *Networks* include all systems, infrastructures, and equipment associated with data, telecommunications, and computer processing assets. *Information* includes various types of proprietary data.

> 2. **Specify loss risk events/vulnerabilities.** Risks or threats are those incidents likely to occur at a site, either due to a history of such events or circumstances in the local environment. They also can be based on the intrinsic value of assets housed or present at a facility or event. A loss risk event can be determined through a vulnerability analysis. The vulnerability analysis should take into consideration anything that could be taken advantage of to carry out a threat. This process should highlight points of weakness and assist in the construction of a framework for subsequent analysis and countermeasures.

> 3. **Establish the probability of loss risk and frequency of events.** *Frequency of events* relates to the regularity of the loss event. For example, if the threat is the assault of patrons at a

---

[10] ASIS International Commission on Guidelines, *General Security Risk Assessment Guideline* (Alexandria, Virginia: ASIS International, 2004).

shopping mall, the frequency would be the number of times the event occurs each day that the mall is open. *Probability of loss risk* is a concept based upon considerations of such issues as prior incidents, trends, warnings, or threats, and such events occurring at the enterprise.

4. **Determine the impact of the events.** The financial, psychological, and related costs associated with the loss of tangible or intangible assets of an organization.

5. **Develop options to mitigate risks.** Identify options available to prevent or mitigate losses through physical, procedural, logical, or related security processes.

6. **Study the feasibility of implementation of options.** Practicality of implementing the options without substantially interfering with the operation or profitability of the enterprise.

7. **Perform a cost/benefit analysis.**

The general approach just presented can help a security planner begin to conceptualize the full range of risk assessment elements. The ASIS guideline, however, obviously is not tailored to the executive protection field. A later section of this chapter discusses the specific elements of an executive protection-oriented risk assessment.

The U.S. Secret Service has also developed tools for risk or threat assessment, which it calls "the process of investigating and analyzing persons and groups who are interested in and capable of attacking public persons."[11] The document titled *Protective Intelligence & Threat Assessment Investigations: A Guide for State and Local Law Enforcement Officials* reports and interprets the findings of the Exceptional Case Study Project. Performed by the U.S. Secret Service, the project examined the thinking and behavior of the 83 persons known to have attacked or come close to attacking prominent public officials and figures in the United States in the

---

[11] Robert Fein and Bryan Vossekuil, *Protective Intelligence & Threat Assessment Investigations: A Guide for State and Local Law Enforcement Officials* (Washington: National Institute of Justice, 1998), available at www.secretservice.gov/ntac/ntac_pi_guide_state.pdf.

past 50 years. The purpose of the project was to examine in detail the lives of assassins and would-be assassins to determine any common traits. Researchers felt that similarities of characteristics, thoughts, or behaviors among past assassins could help law enforcement officials better identify which persons could pose a present threat to public figures.

Among the guide's key points are these:

- *Mental illness only rarely plays a key role in assassination behaviors.* Attacks on prominent persons are the actions of people who see assassination as a rational way to achieve their goals or solve problems. Mostly near-lethal approachers and the great majority of assassins were not mentally ill. None were models of emotional well-being, but relatively few suffered from serious mental illnesses that caused their attack behaviors.

- *Persons who pose an actual threat often do not make threats, especially direct threats.* Although some threateners may pose a real threat, usually they do not. Moreover, those who *pose* threats frequently *do not make* threats. The research found that none of the 83 assassins and attackers communicated a direct threat to the target before their attack. This finding does not mean one should ignore threatening communications, but careful attention should also be paid to identifying, investigating, and assessing anyone whose behaviors suggest that he or she might pose a threat of violence, even if the individual does not communicate direct threats to a target or to the authorities.

- *Attackers and near-lethal approachers had a combination of eight major motives:* to achieve notoriety or fame; bring attention to a personal or public problem; avenge a perceived wrong; end personal pain, be removed from society, or be killed; save the country or the world; develop a special relationship with the target; make money; or bring about political change.

- *Inappropriate or unusual interest, coupled with action, increases the likelihood that the person may pose a threat.* Inappropriate or unusual interest alone is not cause for great alarm, but if the person has also visited the target's home or office or attempted to approach the target in a public place, the case is more serious.

As the document observes:[12]

> Threat assessment or protective intelligence is the process of gathering and assessing information about persons who may have the interest, motive, intention, and capability of mounting attacks against public officials and figures. Gauging the potential threat to and vulnerability of a targeted individual is key to preventing violence. Among criminal justice functions, threat assessment holds great promise for determining vulnerability and guiding interventions in potentially lethal situations.

Although the document was written to aid law enforcement agencies, its observations apply equally well to protective operations in the private sector. An EP specialist can use the report's insights into assassins to watch for potential attackers and to keep protectees out of harm's way. The report's three key observations about assassins are as follows:[13]

Attacks are the product of organized thinking and behavior

> Almost without exception, assassinations, attacks, and near-attacks are neither impulsive nor spontaneous acts. The notion of attacking the President does not leap fully formed into the mind of a person standing at a political rally attended by the President. Ideas of assassination develop over weeks, months, even years, and are stimulated by television and newspaper images, movies, and books. Potential assassins seek out historical information about assassination, the lives of attackers, and the protectors of their targets. They may deliberate about which target—and sometimes targets—to choose. They also may transfer their interest from one target to another....

---

[12] Fein, p. 7.
[13] Fein, pp. 15-20.

Attacks are the means to a goal

Most people who attack others consider violence the means to a goal or a way to solve a problem. The problem may be that the potential perpetrator feels unbearably unhappy, enraged, overwhelmed, or bereft. If the person views violence as an acceptable or permissible solution, the risk of violent action increases....

Motive and target selection are directly connected

Contrary to the general perception, few assassins in the United States—even those targeting major political leaders—have had purely political motives. Other than the Puerto Rican nationalists who attacked President Harry S. Truman in 1950 and Members of Congress in 1954, most recent assassins, attackers, and near-lethal approachers held motives unrelated to politics or political causes. [The Exceptional Case Study Project's] examination of the thinking and behavior of the 83 American attackers and near-lethal approachers identified 8 major motives, most of which are personal.... [See motives listed earlier in this chapter.]

Many attackers and near-lethal approachers craved attention and notoriety, while others acted to bring attention to a particular problem. A number of assailants of public officials and figures were consumed with seeking revenge for perceived injuries or harm. A few attacked or nearly attacked public officials or figures in hopes of being killed by law enforcement or being removed from society by being incarcerated. Several believed that assassinating their target was a way to save the world. Others responded to beliefs or imagined voices that they felt ordered them to attack a national leader. A number of subjects approached a celebrity with a weapon to try to force the target into a special relationship. Finally, a few attacked public officials or figures for money, either because they were paid to kill the target or as part of an attempt to secure ransom money.

Targets are selected on the basis of motive, not primarily because of feelings about or hostility toward a particular target or office. Whether an individual likes a particular elected official may be irrelevant if the individual's motive is to achieve notoriety. "I would have voted for him," said one would-be attacker, "if I hadn't been in jail charged with trying to kill him."

Threat Tracking

One of the most important systems to establish, because of its significant effect on EP planning, is a system for tracking specific threats and security-relevant incidents concerning the principal. Such a system is typically called a threat tracking system, and an EP specialist should encourage the principal's organization to establish a threat tracking system as soon as possible if one is not already in place.

A threat tracking system provides a key ingredient in EP risk assessment: a record of threatening letters, phone calls, other communications, and incidents. That information helps the EP specialist gauge the level of risk faced by the principal. A threat tracking system requires a central collector of threatening communications. Perhaps the principal's executive assistant took notes on a threatening telephone call. Perhaps the mail room staff intercepted a letter containing violent language against the principal. Perhaps the information technology (IT) department caught an e-mail that contained veiled or explicit threats. The communications of greatest concern may well be investigated, while odd but ambiguous communications may only be noted. Regardless, all such communications should be shared with the central collector of threat information, who should be, ideally, the EP specialist.

In the executive protection sphere, threat tracking is an important tool for discerning trends. For example, an adversary or unbalanced person may begin with obnoxious letters, then graduate to odd phone calls, and next begin showing up where he is not welcome. Recordkeeping regarding such events can aid in tracing the person's pattern of behavior and may suggest whether it is moving in a dangerous direction. Moreover, the threats from a single person may be received by various parties at the organization. Each party may think the threat is an isolated incident, but a tracking system would show that the threatening person is actually making many threats. The tracking system should also log suspicious communicators' names into a database and preserve any odd letters. The letters may serve as evidence later.

Traditionally, security-conscious organizations have given bomb threat cards to key receptionists, customer service telephone staff, and executive assistants. The cards contain questions to help the recipient of the call note useful information, such as background noises in the call, the caller's accent, the specificity of the threat, etc. When a threatening call comes in, the recipient of the call can pull out the bomb threat card (which also applies to other threats) and fill in the blanks. A sample of such a card is presented in this book's appendix.

Remarkably, callers have been known to leave threatening voice mails. If the principal's organization develops a means of preserving those messages (rather than deleting them), EP staff may gain yet another valuable source of information.

The strongest predictor of future threats and harmful incidents is the occurrence of threats and harmful incidents in the past. Sometimes past threats are regarded as insignificant, and no security measures are put in place as a response. Inertia is a fact of life. However, the world is dangerous enough for most people, and those who receive threats most likely face an even higher degree of danger. Threats should not be ignored.

In the author's experience, organizations are sometimes surprisingly inactive in response to threatening situations that might affect their executives. In some cases the underpowered response may come from the natural human desire not to face bad news, while in other cases the lack of response may simply result from a failure to put the puzzle pieces together and see the dangerous pattern.

For example, while conducting an executive protection risk assessment for one client organization, the author's firm found that the following events had taken place without a significant security or EP response:

- A few years before the risk assessment, at a national training meeting hosted by the principal's company, an engineer employed by the company walked into a men's room with a large duffel bag. He was followed in and was seen to be donning camouflage clothing and applying face paint. A firearm was found in his bag, and he was taken from the building. Further details of the incident were not recorded in any orderly fashion, and there was no further response to the episode.

- During a personal interview with the risk assessment team, the principal divulged that a few years earlier he had conducted an awkward termination, and the fired employee became angry with him, to the point of almost striking him. Three years after the firing, the principal and his wife were at home when the doorbell rang. At the door was the large son (in his 20s) of the person who had been fired. The agitated son threateningly demanded to know why the executive had fired his father. Such an incident presented a substantial risk to the principal but resulted in no changes to the protection program.

- A non-employee managed to enter the supposedly secure executive floor at the company's headquarters. He was most likely an overly aggressive salesman. The incident probably did not represent a threat, but it showed that an unauthorized person could readily reach the executive office space.

Clearly, some of those events were serious, while others may have posed less of a threat. The lesson, however, is that it is vital to collect information on such events in one location so that their significance can be weighed individually and in total.

Elements of EP Risk Assessment

Executives often live in safer neighborhoods than the average person, but they are more lucrative targets for criminals. Executives tend to travel in greater comfort than the average person, but they also tend to travel more, increasing their exposure to accidents and attacks. Executives may work in safe offices rather than potentially dangerous factories, but to anyone seeking revenge against an employer, executives symbolize the company more than other workers do.

To determine whether an executive needs protection and how best to provide it, an EP risk assessment is needed. Through that process, the EP specialist or an outside consultant examines the executive's risk-attracting characteristics, looking at crime rates for places he or she frequents, studying any threats that might have been made against the executive or the company, assessing the executive's travel habits and conditions, surveying the executive's home and office security, and so on.

Using historical threat information, personal interviews of key persons in the principal's life, site visits, and extensive outside research (including on-line research), the EP specialist (EPS) studies several key categories of information:

- *Executive's exposure to various types of dangers.* These include injury (unintentional); ordinary criminal activity; assassination attempts; threats that are not targeted at the executive but that can affect him or her incidentally (crossfire on the street, hotel fires, etc.); attacks by insane persons, zealots, or disgruntled employees; medical emergencies; and kidnapping (a crime that is more common than most people think).

- *Executive's attractiveness as a target.* Issues include visible signs of significant wealth and the executive's position as head of a controversial organization or an organization that stands as a replacement target for something that is more difficult to attack, such as the United States government or military.

- *Executive's public exposure.* Some executives are widely known by name and face, and much information may be available about them and their families on the Internet. Other executives, just as powerful and well-to-do, may be unknown to the public and succeed in keeping their names out of directories and news articles. In both cases, if the greatest risk comes from employees, shareholders, or protesters who choose their targets after much research, the public recognizability of the principal may not matter as much as his or her symbolic representation of the organization.

- *Security measures currently in place for the principal.* This information is essential, of course, for judging the current level of risk and for planning a prudent response to it.

The information in the preceding categories can be developed by studying the following:

- corporate information exposure
- individual information exposure
- other risk assessment elements
- risk climate
- principal's concerns

The remainder of this chapter examines those five issues.

Corporate Information Exposure

In examining corporate information exposure, the EP specialist researches the degree to which potential adversaries might be aware of the organization, how much information they could obtain about it, and what attitudes they might hold toward it.

Most organizations for which an executive might work have a prominent public profile. Typically, a company is eager for people to learn about its products or services, so it makes itself easy to learn about (for example, in periodicals and on the World Wide

Web) and easy to find (certainly not concealing its telephone number or address).

From a security standpoint, those are negative factors. However, it would be hard for a major corporation to be effective without being well known and easy to contact. These days, only a few organizations maintain a very low profile. Some private foundations or exclusive investment organizations may operate quietly, even without Web sites, but they are the exception. Practically speaking, it is unreasonable to suggest that a principal's organization remove itself from the limelight. Still, it is important to study the degree of public awareness of the organization.

Awareness of a company is not the only issue. Of greater concern is the amount of detailed information one can find about a company. For example, corporate Web sites, press releases, and news accounts may announce upcoming conventions, speeches, business plans, and more. Such sources may divulge the company's involvement in controversial activities (such as oil drilling, animal testing, logging, or defense systems development). When the EP specialist learns how much information is available, he or she can draw conclusions as to what types of adversaries might wish to harm the company, possibly by harming its top executive.

In studying the corporate information exposure of a recent client firm, research uncovered, as usual, a wealth of risk-relevant information about the company. The following list presents types of information that were found, along with reasons that information might cause concern:

- The company manufactures a widespread, useful product that, unfortunately, is suspected of causing cancer and pollution when used improperly. (Some radical environmentalists greatly dislike the company for that reason.)
- A U.S. government Web site lists the company as a polluter. (That designation is enough to put the company in the bad graces of some potential adversaries.)

- The company's Web pages list the corporate officers and their biographies but do not provide photographs of them. However, the company's annual report, downloadable from the Web site, shows the officers' photos. Thus, simple research makes it possible to know which people are in charge of the company, what their backgrounds are, and what they look like. (The listings of names, photographs, and biographies can aid adversaries in target selection and attack planning.)

- The company recently made headlines with the announcement of its plan to purchase a major competitor. Suggestions were made in the press that layoffs might follow. (Such economic impact can spur disgruntled current or former employees or anti-capitalist agitators to undertake dangerous action.)

- In addition, news reports suggested that several of the company's top executives were likely to gain millions of dollars by exercising stock options. (That type of information may further inflame potential adversaries.)

In the case of the company just described, even though some of the information that is publicly available about the company could be of use to adversaries, it was not practical to recommend reducing the company's public profile. At most, the company could consider minimizing its use of photos and biographies of corporate officers. Beyond that, it is too costly in business terms for a company to attempt to hide. Executive protection is meant to further the corporate mission, not impede it.

Individual Information Exposure

One of the key determinants of risk level is how well a principal is known to potential adversaries. Several kinds of threats are increased and facilitated by an adversary's access to information about the principal. For example, information gathering is a key factor in industrial espionage, identity theft, extortion, kidnapping of family members or relatives, and efforts to do the principal bodily harm. Obtaining one piece of information makes it easier to obtain others. Dedicated adversaries can learn the names of schools attended by the principal or family members, obtain school yearbook photographs (which can be parlayed into other information), and generally build a thorough profile of an individual.

Therefore, the EP specialist should examine any information about the executive that is available to inquisitive members of the public. Sources include annual reports, company promotional materials, newspaper and magazine articles, industry directories, the Internet, and even waste paper sent to unsecured trash bins. By finding out, on an ongoing basis, what a potential adversary could learn about the principal, it is possible to stay a step ahead in planning a defense.

The Web makes it almost effortless for researchers, both benevolent and malevolent, to read current and past articles about any topic or person they choose. Even a cursory Web search, for many executives, discloses their spouse's name, whether they have children, and what city they live in. It is important to remember the first two W's in WWW. The web truly is worldwide, so adversaries in other parts of the globe can research an executive just as easily as the executive's next-door neighbor can.

In addition, information seekers can learn more detailed information about their targets by paying a small fee (typically a few dollars per record) for such information as the following:

- vehicle title records
- property records
- voter registration records
- birth and death records
- genealogical information
- certain tax records
- cell phone records

Information of that sort can also be gathered through visits to local record repositories, such as city halls or county courthouses. Another common practice is simply to ask a target's friends and neighbors for information, using various pretexts.

In researching a principal's information exposure, the EP specialist should look for sources that divulge any of the following:

- addresses (of primary or secondary homes)
- telephone numbers
- photographs
- family information
- degree of wealth
- involvement in any controversial activities, causes, or issues

Basically, in assessing risk, it is useful to know what information is available that could arouse envy, hatred, or revenge or could help an adversary locate and harm the principal or his or her loved ones.

Information exposure also applies in-house. Risk assessment research should look into the degree of privacy accorded to the principal's schedule. An interview with an executive assistant might divulge the fact that after hours someone (such as a member of the cleaning crew) could read the principal's calendar to learn about the principal's upcoming movements. It may even be the case that the principal's schedule is posted, though not in full detail, on the company intranet for all or some employees to view.

Protectees can take several steps to reduce their information exposure. They can have their telephone numbers unlisted, decline to discuss their families and strive to keep them from being photographed for magazine articles, and maintain a low profile in activities that might tend to spur adversaries to action. Still, an active, prominent executive can hardly afford to disappear, and much of the most sensitive information cannot be concealed anyway. For example, often the most significant Internet information available about principals is their income or personal wealth, and that is information that officers of publicly held corporations cannot conceal.

Emerging Information Sources

Over time, despite various legal and technological privacy protections, adversaries find it easier and easier to gain information about a principal. For many reasons, good and ill, whole new categories of information are becoming susceptible to discovery or interception. Various branches of government, medical facilities, financial institutions, and even retail stores collect increasing amounts of information that an adversary could use to harm the principal. The information might facilitate a dangerous attack, or it might simply be used to embarrass the principal and his or her organization.

A particular challenge for EP specialists is that the ways of obtaining information about a principal are constantly changing. Thus, not only is more information about principals being stored in more and more places, but new means of accessing that information develop constantly. In recent years, the security field has become aware of the information loss risks related to a principal's garbage; notebook computer; mobile telephone; personal digital assistant (PDA); e-mail accounts; family Web pages; phishing, spoofing, and pharming;[14] and other sources. EP specialists should routinely keep their eyes and ears open to discern upcoming sources of trouble from a privacy perspective. The new sources of information exposure may grow out of the world's

---

[14] Phishing refers to the use of official-looking but fraudulent e-mails designed to convince consumers to divulge personal information. Spoofing is the use of false Web sites designed to do the same. Pharming is a malicious Web redirection that sends a user who is trying to reach a legitimate commercial site to a criminal's spoofed site, usually by means of worms, Trojan horses, or other techniques that attack the browser address bar and exploit vulnerabilities in operating systems and Domain Name Service systems.

ever-changing technology, or they may simply bloom from a criminal's ingenuity.

News accounts from the Netherlands describe an uncommon but potentially effective means of gathering information about a principal: searching pharmacy records. One terrorist organization in the Netherlands is called the Hofstad Group—a cell of militant Muslims that has been linked to plots to attack Amsterdam's Schiphol Airport and a nuclear power plant and to assassinate Dutch politicians and officials. (Its most famous member is Mohammed Bouyeri, who was sentenced to life in prison on July 26, 2005, for the November 2004 slaying of filmmaker Theo van Gogh.). In 2005, a member of the Hofstad group was charged with attempting to obtain information about two Dutch politicians *via their pharmacy records.* The accused allegedly asked her sister, an employee of a pharmacy used by members of the country's parliament, for the addresses of Conservative Party leader Jozias van Aartsen and Home Affairs Minister Johan Remkes.

Even for people who attempt to maintain a low profile by keeping their telephone numbers (and hence their addresses) unlisted in public directories, pharmacy records are likely to contain their real names, addresses, telephone numbers, and social security numbers, in addition to any sensitive or embarrassing medical information.

Ethically and legally, pharmacists may not share that information with unauthorized parties. However, pharmacy employees could potentially be encouraged, bribed, coerced, or tricked into releasing a principal's private information. This is not to single out pharmacies as a particular weak link in the information chain, but only to point out that any repository of information can be compromised. The bottom line is that the EP specialist should (1) encourage the principal to restrict the release of private information wherever possible and (2) be aware of the types of information that could potentially be compromised and plan appropriate protective responses. For any principal, information exposure is a risk that can never be eliminated, only minimized and managed.

Information Exposure Case Study

The following is the type of information that might turn up in a normal search of a corporate executive's information exposure. It is a fictitious example based on numerous risk assessments that the author has performed. None of the information items would represent, to an adversary, shocking or irresistible information. Moreover, the executive's information exposure, overall, is typical for someone in his position. What is significant is the total picture that might attract an adversary or help one develop a plan to harm the principal.

The fictitious search regarding the information exposure of Mr. Smith finds the following:

- Mr. Smith is widely recognized in public, according to Mrs. Smith and Mr. Smith's executive assistant. Mr. Smith is easy to spot at conferences and restaurants, and people routinely step up and introduce themselves to him. On a few occasions, such meetings have had a tone that was negative, though not plainly threatening.

- Mr. Smith is often mentioned or pictured in newspapers and magazines in connection with his role as an executive of a major corporation. A few articles have mentioned that he is married with children, have published family members' ages and names, and have included photos of Mr. Smith with his family.

- Many civic organizations have presented Mr. Smith with awards, which they publicize with press releases and pages on their Web sites.

- Mr. Smith's picture and page-long biography are displayed at the corporate Web site.

- *Forbes* magazine lists Mr. Smith's income as $2.9 million in its current list, ranking Mr. Smith in 289th place among

U.S. executives. In the preceding several years, he was also listed within the top 500.

- Numerous financial sites on the Web show Mr. Smith holding 400,000 shares of his employer's stock. Those same sites show that he has sold over $6 million worth of stock in the last two years.

- Aerial photos of the Smith house are readily available, at no cost, on-line. Such photos could help an adversary locate the house, see what surrounds it, and plan approach and escape routes.

- Mr. Smith's home telephone number and address are available on-line at various phone directory sites.

The information that is readily available about Mr. Smith shows him to be a relatively wealthy person with a family living at a known location. Since pictures of Mr. Smith and his family are also available, an adversary can be assumed to be able to find and track either the principal or his family. Most of the information cannot be retracted from the public sphere, but by learning what information is available, the EP specialist can better devise a protection strategy.

Other Risk Assessment Elements

Studying corporate and individual information exposure is only part of the EP risk assessment. Many other topics must be investigated if a complete risk assessment is to be performed. Again, all this research is geared toward discovering the following:

- executive's exposure to various types of dangers
- executive's attractiveness as a target
- executive's public exposure
- security measures currently in place for the principal

The way to discover information in the preceding categories is to visit the relevant physical locations and to interview people who work with and around the principal. The following are some important steps to take and questions to answer:

- *Consider who would want to harm the executive.* How are adversaries gaining information about him? How likely are the various threats? What controversial institutions or causes does the executive represent?

- *Study the organization's threat file, if one exists.* If one does not exist, the EP specialist should work to establish one.

- *Study the principal's exposure to workplace violence.* Does the principal conduct high-stress employment terminations? Does the principal clearly symbolize the company to anyone who would want to harm the organization? Does the principal participate in adversarial negotiations with a union? Is there a history of workplace violence at the principal's main office or at plants to which he or she may travel? Are any business developments expected that might increase the likelihood of workplace violence, such as layoffs?

- *Obtain information on crime levels and types from local police contacts or state crime analysis experts.* The section titled "Risk Climate" below discusses the study of crime rates.

- *Become informed as to whether people who match the executive's profile have been the object of any attacks.* Have other executives in the industry been targeted? Have principals who have similar degrees of wealth and engage in similar activities been targeted by adversaries, whether protesters, financially motivated criminals, or others? Have people who match the principal's profile been kidnapped, at home or abroad?

- *Attempt to discover the principal's primary concerns.* Have there been suspicious incidents around the house? Is the principal concerned about security at his or her vacation home? Is the principal worried about the safety of his or her children or spouse?

- *Examine security measures at the executive's place of work.* Does the building have adequate control of access to the main office areas and the executive suite? Are closed-circuit television systems, intrusion alarm systems, panic alarms, and safe rooms (if needed) in place? Who are the other tenants in the building, if any? What is the quality of building security staff—are they properly trained, sufficiently aware of EP requirements, and available to help in an emergency? If the executive drives himself or herself to work, is secure parking available? Is the route taken from either the parking area or the drop-off area (if the executive is driven to work) secure? Are members of the public allowed into the building, for example during shareholder meetings? Is the executive's mail examined by either mail room staff or the executive assistant for suspicious signs? Do staffers know what to do if they find a suspicious piece of mail? Are adequate first aid supplies, including automated external defibrillators, readily available and in good condition? What is the history of crime in the area surrounding the office building? What is the speed and quality of response by the local law enforcement agency, fire department, and emergency medical response unit? Is the office located near other potential targets, so that it could suffer collateral damage in an attack against those targets?

- *Study the security posture of the principal's primary and, if applicable, secondary homes.* What is the crime situation around the homes? What is the speed and quality of response by the relevant law enforcement agency, fire department, and emergency medical response unit? Does the home have the right burglar alarm system, exterior lighting, locks, security signs, first aid supplies, fire extinguishers, and other protective measures? Do members of the household staff know that they should not divulge unnecessary information about the family or allow unauthorized persons into the home? Does the executive pass through dangerous areas on the commute to work? Does the executive engage in personal activities that may put him or her in harm's way or inflame potential adversaries?

- *Gather information on the principal's travel habits.* How often does the principal travel? Are some of the destinations dangerous? Does the principal travel by commercial or private aircraft? If private, what security measures are taken at the fixed-base operators (FBOs, or private flight terminals) used by the principal, what security measures are taken by the flight crews, and what security and safety equipment is aboard the aircraft? On travel, does the principal ever have to perform tasks that could lead to dangerous reactions, such as firing a local plant manager? Are the principal's travel plans announced in advance, either within or outside the company?

The preceding steps and questions are not the totality of necessary inquiry, but they should provide some idea of the range and depth of investigation involved in an EP risk assessment.

Crime Climate

Several types of crime statistics have a general bearing on the risk faced by the principal. The EP specialist should gather information about crime around the principal's office, primary home, any secondary homes, other work sites visited, and places frequented during non-work hours.

Crime statistics are a very generalized type of information. They provide an idea of the risk faced by an average person in the geographical area considered. They do not provide tailored information about the risk faced by the principal. That risk level rises or falls depending on whether the principal is specifically targeted (by a pro-tester, for example), how the principal travels through the defined geographical area (in a protected car, for example), and other factors. Still, crime statistics give a general idea of the relative likelihood that the principal could be harmed through street crime and terrorism.

According to recent FBI figures, crime levels are, for the most part, down slightly:[15]

> As a whole, law enforcement agencies throughout the Nation reported a decrease of 0.5 percent in the number of violent crimes brought to their attention in the first half of 2005 when compared to figures reported for the first six months of 2004. The violent crime category includes murder, forcible rape, robbery, and aggravated assault. The number of property crimes in the United States from January to June of 2005 decreased 2.8 percent when compared to data from the same time period in 2004. Property crimes include burglary, larceny-theft, and motor vehicle theft. Arson is also a property crime, but data for arson are not included in property crime totals. Figures for the first half of 2005 indicated that arson decreased 5.6 percent when compared to 2004 figures.

Another source describes the general risk of death or injury due to terrorism. Obviously, a principal who is specifically targeted by terrorists or routinely travels to areas where terror attacks are concentrated would face a greater-than-average risk. Still, there is plenty of opportunity to be harmed by a terror attack simply by being in the wrong place at the wrong time.

A CNN article notes the following:[16]

> There were 3,192 terrorist attacks in 2004, with 28,433 people killed, wounded, or kidnapped, according to an estimate from the U.S. National Counterterrorism Center (NCTC). The numbers represent a revision, as the U.S. government had stated in April that only 651 "significant" attacks occurred during 2004, killing 1,907 people. Unlike the figures released in April, the NCTC's numbers include attacks that were of a

---

[15] "Preliminary Semiannual Uniform Crime Report, Jan.-June 2005," Washington: Federal Bureau of Investigation, 2005.

[16] David Ensor, "U.S. Raises Estimate for Terror Attacks," CNN Web site, July 5, 2005, available at www.cnn.com/2005/US/07/05/terror. site/?section=cnn_latest.

domestic nature. The April numbers had left out several notable incidents, including the February 2004 bombing of a Philippine superferry and the August 2004 suicide attacks that destroyed two Russian airliners…. Terrorism as defined by the NCTC involves the use of violence against noncombatants or civilians to make a political point. Thus, the NCTC says that attacks against U.S. soldiers in Iraq do not count as terrorism, but attacks like the 2000 bombing of the USS Cole in which military personnel are attacked in a "non-combat setting" will be included in the statistics.

EP specialists can consult several useful sources to stay abreast of terrorism risk. (Statistically, terrorism is not the greatest risk most executives face, but it is a risk about which the EP specialist should remain well informed.) The Web site of the Overseas Security Advisory Council[17] (a project of the U.S. Department of State) is one good source of information related to terrorism and travel safety. *Security Management* magazine,[18] published by ASIS International, features a monthly column called "Intelligence," which often presents terrorism figures from the MIPT Knowledge Base.[19]

International, national, regional, and state crime statistics are useful for spotting broad crime trends and making comparisons across large areas. However, individuals spend their time, and face their risks, in specific, local jurisdictions, not broad geographic areas. Therefore, local crime data are more useful for assessing the risk to individuals and for tailoring protective strategies.

To obtain local crime statistics for areas in which the principal lives and works, the EP specialist may have to visit the relevant law enforcement agencies in those jurisdictions and speak to crime analysis officers, but there is also a good chance that the desired information is available on-line.

In New York City, for example, data are available on both the citywide and police precinct level. Therefore, it is possible to

---

[17] See www.ds-osac.org.
[18] See www.securitymanagement.com.
[19] Memorial Institute for the Prevention of Terrorism, www.tkb.org.

know the crime situation in the area immediately surrounding the principal's office and, if he or she lives in the city, at home. The following table shows the type of information available on-line from the New York City Police Department:

Volume 12 Number 38			**CompStat**								**Midtown South Precinct**	
Report Covering the Week of 09/19/2005 Through 09/25/2005												
Crime Complaints												
	Week to Date			28 Day			Year to Date*			2 Year	4 Year	12 Year
	2005	2004	% Change	2005	2004	% Change	2005	2004	% Chg	% Chg	% Chg (2001)	% Chg (1993)
Murder	0	0	****.*	0	0	****.*	1	1	0.0	-66.6	-66.6	-88.8
Rape	2	1	100.0	2	3	-33.3	8	16	-50.0	-11.1	0.0	-75.7
Robbery	6	6	0.0	30	23	30.4	239	235	1.7	-12.7	-38.8	-87.4
Fel. Assault	1	5	-80.0	15	30	-50.0	126	186	-32.2	-37.6	-46.3	-74.6
Burglary	13	8	62.5	41	47	-12.7	434	444	-2.2	-28.7	-30.2	-78.0
Gr. Larceny	64	72	-11.1	239	246	-2.8	2,250	2,393	-5.9	-10.2	-26.0	-67.9
G.L.A.	2	0	****.*	3	4	-25.0	45	46	-2.1	4.6	-45.1	-82.8
TOTAL	**88**	**92**	**-4.35**	**330**	**353**	**-6.52**	**3,103**	**3,321**	**-6.56**	**-14.92**	**-29.20**	**-73.48**

An EP specialist does not have to be a statistician to interpret such data. The figures in the NYPD chart show declines in most crime categories. Nevertheless, in 2005, as of September 25, the Midtown South Precinct had experienced one murder, 239 robberies, and 126 felonious assaults. Knowledge of crime levels and trends can help the EP specialist establish an appropriate level of protection: not too little and not too much.

Principal's Concerns

In a risk assessment, some threats can be evaluated objectively from the outside (for example, by the EP specialist or an EP consulting firm), yet it is also worthwhile to find out what the principal's main concerns are from his or her own point of view. Often, the principal has never told the organization's EP operation or security staff what worries him or her the most. A principal may not know everything about executive protection, but he or she is likely to have inside knowledge and experience that no one else has. The following examples are typical of the types of concerns that have been uncovered in interviews with executives who were the subjects of formal risk assessments:

- One principal expressed concern over the number of flights he had to take in small, unsteady aircraft, arriving at teeming airport terminals in developing countries, where he stood out as an obvious target. He was also concerned about the openness of his organization's headquarters and the possibility of an armed, disgruntled employee causing harm.

- Another executive worried about security during travel to Latin America, a region with an especially high rate of kidnapping. Specifically, he asked how one could be sure that a local security person at the destination would not be bought off by kidnappers.

- An executive said he is concerned that public knowledge of his income may put his family at risk.

- Another executive was deeply concerned about a tense, gun-brandishing, possible attempted robbery or kidnapping incident that he had recently experienced in a Latin American country. His car had been blocked in at a toll booth, and armed men in the truck behind him stood up, began shouting, and pointed their guns at his car. His security detail told him to lie down in the vehicle; they exchanged words with the apparent attackers and then were able to drive him away to safety. It was unclear to both the executive and his security staff whether the apparent attackers were police or simply dressed as police.

- Another executive was worried about the possibility of violent reactions to several employment terminations for which he was responsible.

- An executive had been the victim of a violent kidnapping attempt at his home. Although the attempt was not successful, the executive was injured and was determined not to let such an attack happen again.

Linking It All Together

Risk assessment is the basis of executive protection. It gives the EP specialist the tools to decide whether protection is needed, in what circumstances, by what means, and to what extent. It is important to note that the risk assessment is not a one-time exercise. The EP specialist must continually collect and analyze data to determine the principal's vulnerability and gauge the range and level of threats that must be defended against. Because the risk level of any given principal changes over time, the EP specialist should be prepared to be flexible and realistic in his or her security approach.

Complacency is the enemy of good executive protection. Common errors include the following, all of which are based on complacency and a failure to keep up to date on risks and protective measures:

- failure to detect a surveillance
- failure to react to an assault
- failure to acknowledge and respond to a known threat
- failure to keep the protective detail alert and creative

EP specialists should keep in mind that potential attackers choose the time, the place, and the method of their attack. The adversary only has to succeed once, while the EP specialist has to succeed every time. The advantage that attackers hold stems from the following factors:

- They choose the target.
- They learn where the target is going to be.
- They select and obtain a weapon.
- They survey the security in place.
- They develop an attack plan.
- They consider whether and how to escape.
- They choose the moment of attack.

In view of those factors, the EP specialist should focus on three words: predict, prevent, protect. The protective effort must attempt to predict attacks and other hazards, prevent them, and, failing that, protect the principal if an attack or hazard materializes.

Related to the need for ongoing risk assessment is the need for different protection plans when the risk level changes. In addition to developing a protection plan that meets current risk levels, the EP specialist should develop a written plan for a higher level of security measures that can be put in place when the threat level temporarily spikes upward. (For example, the principal may oversee employee layoffs, handle a difficult termination, or become known as a wealthy person after exercising stock options. Any of those changes could boost the risk level and require stronger security measures to be put in place temporarily.) A written plan makes it easier to implement higher-level security measures quickly, without wasting time, when the risk level jumps higher than normal. Security measures could be upgraded in several ways. For example, an EP specialist might begin to accompany the principal on some local outings, a security driver might be arranged for the principal, a protected vehicle might be leased, or travel to dangerous locations might be curtailed.

After conducting the initial risk assessment, and by keeping up-to-date on changing risk factors, the EP specialist can intelligently plan security measures tailored to the principal's needs, without overdoing or underdoing the security effort.

4.
Means of Attack and Lessons Learned

When examined carefully, case studies can offer the EP specialist several valuable benefits. Accounts of actual attacks against principals can provide the following:

- evidence to show reluctant protectees that the risk of attack, in many forms and in many places, is real

- an opportunity to study how and sometimes why adversaries committed particular attacks—that is, their methods, timing, weapons, planning, surveillance, and motivation

- an opportunity to learn from others' mistakes or misfortunes—in other words, any errors in risk assessment, physical security measures, EP policies, or countersurveillance

Few case studies contain all the foregoing elements, but all provide an opportunity for learning about what went wrong, what went right, and how protection could be provided better in the future. Moreover, because of the history of copycat behavior (for example, in such matters as carjacking and express kidnapping[20]), case studies are worth examining for the possible trendsetting effect that an incident may have.

The Bomb

Sad to say, one expects to read about bombing attacks in the Middle East, where terrorists regularly detonate explosives in cars and on their bodies in order to kill innocent bystanders. Of course, well-known bombings have also taken place in Madrid (March 11, 2004) and London (July 7, 2005, with another, similar but unsuccessful attack on July 23, 2005).

Perhaps because newspapers focus on the numerous spectacular bombings that take place overseas, many people are unaware of the extent of bombing in the United States. In general, U.S. bombings are directed at specific targets (people and buildings), rather than being designed simply to harm as many people as possible, as appears to be the Middle East model.

Figures on bombings are compiled by the Bureau of Alcohol, Tobacco, Firearms and Explosives, which is a division of the U.S. Department of Homeland Security. The following table is based on the latest available data:

---

[20] Express kidnapping is short-term kidnapping for an amount of money that can be obtained quickly. In recent years, express kidnapping has become common in Latin America.

Explosive Incidents Report for Bombing January 2003 to December 2003				
Bombing Type	**Total**	**Injured**	**Killed**	**Damage**
Actual	220	19	5	$506,912
Actual incendiary	74	10	1	$4,630,900
Attempted	43	0	0	$1,500
Attempted incendiary	24	0	0	$2,200
Premature explosion	25	26	1	$267,000
Total:	386	55	7	$5,408,512
Source: http://www.atf.treas.gov/aexis2/bombingrpts/bombings2003.pdf				

As the table shows, in 2003 in the United States, 294 successful bombing attacks took place, killing seven persons, injuring 55, and causing over $5 million in damage. In addition, 92 other bombings were attempted but failed for various reasons. The total number of attacks and attempted attacks—386—is much greater than most people probably imagine.

Although bombing is not the most common means by which executives are attacked, it is certainly a serious risk that EP specialists should work to minimize. Protecting a principal from a bombing attack (if the risk assessment suggests that the principal is a potential target) is challenging, as bombs can be delivered by many means and detonated by timers or from a distance. In other words, the adversary may never come into contact with the principal or the EP specialist.

Some bombs, of course, are delivered through the mail. Concern for mail screening jumped at the time of the 2001 anthrax letters. However, since then, many corporate mail rooms have let down their guard.

This section describes several bombing attacks against protectees and offers lessons learned that may help other EP specialists better protect their principals. The accounts are compiled from numerous news sources.

A checklist on how to respond when a bomb threat is called into a workplace is presented in the appendix.

Risk of Being Next to a Target

On May 9, 2004, Chechen President Akhmad Kadyrov and at least five others died in an explosion at a stadium in Grozny, the Chechen capital. The explosion, which came from a land mine planted under stadium seats, also killed the chairman of the Chechen state council, two of Kadyrov's protective staff, a journalist, and a child. Another 56 people were wounded, including General Valery Baranov, the commander of Russian forces in Chechnya.

The stadium was crowded with people celebrating Victory Day, which marks the defeat of Nazi Germany in World War II. The blast happened beneath the VIP stand where political and military leaders were reviewing a military parade.

A spokesman for the Chechen Interior Ministry said the bomb may have been buried in concrete as much as three months earlier while the stadium was undergoing a renovation. He added that detailed security checks had been conducted before the event.

Lessons Learned. Few business executives or wealthy persons would be the object of a bombing attack that required planting a mine in concrete three months before the target was expected to attend an event. However, many business executives or wealthy persons could periodically find themselves in the company of political leaders who might be targeted by attackers willing to engage in such long-range planning.

EP specialists should help their protectees understand the risks of spending time around people who are likely targets of attack. An EP specialist probably would be unable to control the security of an event like the Grozny bombing—security would be in the hands of government or military planners. However, like the September 11, 2001, terrorist attack against the World Trade Center towers in New York City, the Grozny bombing shows that even if an EP specialist cannot prevent an attack, he or she should still have a plan for removing the principal to safety afterwards.

American Hotels in High-Risk Locations

On November 9, 2005, three hotels in Amman, Jordan, experienced terrorist bombings. According to news accounts, about 9:00 pm at the Grand Hyatt hotel, explosives detonated on the ground floor, killing more than 20 persons. Minutes later, at the Radisson SAS hotel, another bomb detonated at a wedding party in the banquet hall, killing at least 20 persons. A few minutes after that, a car packed with explosives blew up outside the Days Inn hotel. In total, approximately 56 people died and almost 100 were wounded. Responsibility for the attack was claimed by the group known as al Qaeda in Iraq.

According to BBC News:[21]

> The claim from al-Qaeda in Iraq appeared on a website generally used to post such announcements.
>
> It said the hotels were targeted because they had become favourites with "American and Israeli intelligence and other Western European governments".
>
> Jordan, a key US ally in the Middle East, has become a base for Westerners who fly in and out of Iraq for work and has long been regarded as a prime target for attack, correspondents say.

Lessons Learned. This case shows the dilemma an EP specialist may face when recommending lodging overseas. Traditionally, in many parts of the world, hotels that are owned or operated by U.S. lodging corporations have been considered a smart choice, given their reputation for better fire safety and physical

---

[21] "Al-Qaeda claims Jordan attacks," BBC News on-line, November 10, 2005, http://news.bbc.co.uk/1/hi/world/middle_east/4423714.stm.

security than many other hotels. However, in areas where buildings associated with the United States may have a high risk of being targeted by bombers, it may make more sense for the EP specialist to recommend a high-quality hotel that offers good fire safety and physical security but is not obviously associated with the United States.

This case therefore demonstrates the importance of conducting a risk assessment or advance research of each place a principal may visit. At some destinations, it may make the most sense to lodge the principal in a high-end hotel operated by a U.S. corporation. At other destinations, the high quality of the hotel may be outweighed by its reputation as a U.S.-related property.

Another lesson is that dying is not the only risk—approximately twice as many people were wounded in the attacks as were killed. If the principal is wounded, will the EP specialist know where to take him or her for medical treatment? Does the EP specialist have a plan for bringing a seriously injured principal home?

Unabomber

Bomb attacks against ideological opponents and business competitors have occurred often in the United States. In some cases, the attacker chose the victim because of a specific dispute with the person; in other cases, the victim was selected because he or she merely represented a cause that the bomber opposed; and in many cases, because of the indiscriminate nature of a bomb's destructive force, the victim had no relation to the bomber's mission but just happened to be in the wrong place at the wrong time.

Such events continue, year in and year out, as is shown by the statistics given earlier from the Bureau of Alcohol, Tobacco, Firearms and Explosives. The most famous series of bomb attacks against businesspeople is the 18-year string of attacks by Theodore Kaczynski, also known as the Unabomber. The following timeline from CNN shows the range of his attacks:[22]

> For 18 years, the FBI struggled to find the person responsible for a string of bombing attacks that killed three people and injured 23. Agents gave the case the code name "Unabom" because universities and airlines were the early targets.
>
> **May 25-26, 1978.** A package found in a parking lot at the University of Illinois at Chicago is brought to Northwestern University in Evanston because of the return address. It explodes the next day, when a campus police officer opens it. He suffers minor injuries.
>
> **May 9, 1979.** Northwestern University graduate student John Harris is injured by a bomb left at the school's Technological Institute. He is not seriously hurt.
>
> **Nov. 15, 1979.** A bomb explodes in a mailbag in the cargo hold of an American Airlines flight traveling from Chicago to Washington. Twelve people suffer smoke inhalation. The plane makes an emergency landing at Dulles Airport near Washington.
>
> **June 10, 1980.** United Airlines President Percy Wood receives cuts and burns from a package bomb disguised as a book and delivered by mail to his home in Lake Forest, Illinois, near Chicago.
>
> **Oct. 8, 1981.** A maintenance worker finds a bomb in a business classroom at the University of Utah in Salt Lake City. It is defused by police, and no one is injured.
>
> **May 5, 1982.** Janet Smith, a secretary at Vanderbilt University in Nashville, Tennessee, is injured when she opens a package addressed to a professor.
>
> **July 2, 1982.** Professor Diogenes Angelakos picks up a small box with wires on top in a faculty lounge at the University of California at Berkeley. The electrical engineering and computer science teacher is injured when the pipe bomb device explodes.
>
> **May 15, 1985.** U.C. Berkeley engineering graduate student John Hauser has the fingers on his right hand blown off when he opens a plastic box with a bomb inside.
>
> **June 13, 1985.** A package mailed to the Boeing Co. in Auburn, Washington, on May 8 is discovered and safely disarmed.

---

[22] From www.cnn.com/US/9604/11/unabomb_timeline/.

Nov. 15, 1985. Two people are injured by a package mailed to James O'Connell, a psychology professor at the University of Michigan at Ann Arbor. O'Connell, who was standing nearby, wasn't hurt.

Dec. 11, 1985. Hugh Scrutton, 38, is killed when a bomb placed inside a paper bag explodes. Scrutton spotted the bag outside, near the rear entrance of his computer rental store in Sacramento, California.

Feb. 20, 1987. The owner of a computer store in Salt Lake City, Utah, is injured when a bomb left in a paper bag explodes by the store's rear entrance.

June 22, 1993. Charles Epstein, a geneticist at the University of California at San Francisco, loses several fingers when a bomb sent to his Tiburon home explodes. The bomb was inside a padded envelope.

June 24, 1993. In New Haven, Connecticut, Yale University computer science professor David Gelernter is disfigured by a bomb that explodes in his hands at the school's computer science center.

Dec. 10, 1994. Advertising executive Thomas Mosser, 50, is killed when he opens a package bomb sent to his North Caldwell, New Jersey, home.

Apr. 24, 1995. Timber industry lobbyist Gilbert P. Murray, 47, is killed opening a package bomb in his Sacramento office. The package was addressed to the person Murray replaced as president of the California Forestry Association.

Lessons Learned. An EP specialist who wants to protect a principal from attacks like those made by the Unabomber could take action in two primary categories: (1) risk assessment and (2) mail screening. Regarding risk assessment, the EP specialist should routinely conduct research to determine who might want to harm the principal. Such research might include interviews with office staff, customer service representatives, and whoever maintains the organization's threat file; news research to discover trends or movements that might see the principal in a negative light; and crime research to learn about recent attacks against people matching, to some degree, the profile of the principal.

Regarding mail screening, there may be much that the EP specialist can do. Security-conscious businesses use some or all of the following steps to keep dangerous mail from reaching executives:

- arrange for their mail room staff to be trained in recognizing suspicious packages
- post mail security posters throughout the mail room
- x-ray all mail that will be delivered to the principal
- mark all inspected mail with a special mark so the principal or the principal's assistants will know the mail has been checked

The following box describes mail security resources available through the United States Postal Service. A primer on mail bomb security, produced by the United States Postal Inspection Service, is included in the appendix.

Security Resources from the United States Postal Service

The U.S. Postal Service calls mail centers or mail rooms "a major gateway into any business or government agency." The following are some of the security resources the USPS provides to help businesses protect themselves:

Suspicious Mail Poster	Mail Center Security Handbook
http://www.usps.com/communications/news/security/suspiciousmail.htm	http://www.usps.com/cpim/ftp/pubs/pub166.pdf
Tips to protect a business, its mailroom, and its employees	Detailed manual addressing weapons of mass destruction, threats, mail bombs, and employee safety
Mail Tampering Poster	**Best Practices for Mail Center Security**
http://www.usps.com/communications/news/security/mailtampering.htm	Tips and guidelines compiled from postal, government, and private industry mail centers.
Poster to discourage mail tampering	The nearest U.S. Postal Inspector can be found through the following office locator page: http://www.usps.com/ncsc/locators/find-is.html.

The Gun

Although the assassination of President John F. Kennedy in 1963 took place from a long distance, most other attacks against leaders, executives, or other principals have been carried out at short range. In fact, most such shootings have taken place within a 9-foot radius of the principal—an area that EP specialists call the circle of death.

Attack by Former Employee

Four years after being laid off, a former employee is alleged to have returned to take revenge on his former employer:[23]

> Tragedy can be all the more disturbing when it makes little, if no sense. The recent murder of an executive at a subsidiary of the brewer, Heineken Holding, has certainly left many observers scratching their heads.
>
> Frank Stultjens, finance director for Heineken subsidiary Brasseries de Bourbon, died after being shot at the unit's Christmas party on the French island of La Reunion....
>
> [D]etectives suspect the alleged killer, who died when he was apprehended and shot by police officers, was a disaffected former employee.... The ex-employee who is now a suspect had in fact left Heineken's unit four years ago and had not been a member of management. "He didn't even know Frank," [a colleague] said. "[Frank Stultjens] had just moved in October this year."

Lessons Learned. Several EP issues emerge from an analysis of this case. First, EP specialists should consider whether off-site venues for corporate functions are as secure as corporate headquarters. The principal may travel to work in a protected vehicle and spend the day inside the secure executive core of the office, but if an evening event takes place in a significantly less secure location, it may be necessary to provide the principal with in-person protection or perhaps to upgrade the security provided at the event site.

Second, it is unknown whether anyone was tracking threats

---

[23] Parmy Olson, "Heineken Unit CFO Is Shot and Killed," www.forbes.com, December 19, 2005.

that came to the company. Threat tracking is truly a necessity in executive protection. It seems likely that a laid-off employee who later murdered a corporate executive at an off-site Christmas party may have expressed his anger to someone at some point in the four years between those events. Perhaps he made telephone calls, perhaps he wrote letters, or perhaps he muttered about his plans to a former colleague—who may even have given him information on the party's location. In any case, an EP specialist should make sure he or she knows about any acrimonious employment separations or communications of concern. Such techniques as "stay-away" orders could be used to help security staff keep a threatener away from the principal.

Third, if the risk assessment showed a current threat, it might be prudent to have guests and workers pass through an airport-style magnetometer to check for firearms.

Fourth, the EP specialist should again be sure, at all times, of the location of the nearest hospital to which the executive could be taken if injured.

Attack by Disgruntled Customer

Just as former employees with grievances against a company may attack a top executive as a symbol of the company, so too may deeply aggrieved customers. A recent example follows:[24]

> Friends and business associates are mourning the violent death of a prominent Calgarian, shot in his high-rise office early yesterday. Police and EMS were called to the 12th floor offices of Morbank Financial Inc. at 635 8 Ave. S.W. about 8 a.m. after a co-worker discovered company president Jack Beauchamp had been shot in the head and chest....

> Morbank, a mortgage lending company, was founded by Beauchamp in 1998.

> Hours after the shooting, someone was taken into custody, said [police]: "At 11:19, members of the Calgary police tacti-

---

[24] Dave Breakenridge and Pablo Fernandez, "Executive shot dead," *Calgary Sun*, January 17, 2006.

cal unit arrested a person for uttering threats and he will be interviewed." [Police] could not confirm the threats were made against Beauchamp, but sources said there had been documented threats made against him. The 52-year-old man was taken in for questioning.

The next day, the history of the situation began to unfold:[25]

Jack Beauchamp, who by all accounts was an affable Calgary banker, had received threatening e-mails for months leading up to his shooting and death Monday morning in a downtown office tower, police said yesterday.

A 52-year-old Calgary man, who was taken into police custody for questioning just hours after Mr. Beauchamp's body was found lying on the floor outside his office at Morbank Financial Inc., was charged yesterday with criminal harassment....

Acting Staff Sergeant Chris Matthews told reporters yesterday that co-workers and family members told police that Mr. Beauchamp had expressed concerns to them about e-mails dating back to November, which made threats to himself and his family.

Police also wouldn't say how [the man arrested] knew Mr. Beauchamp. However, local media reported that Morbank turned down [the suspect's] application for a mortgage....

Officers were still trying to determine if Mr. Beauchamp filed a formal complaint with police about the allegedly threatening e-mails.

Lessons Learned. This case involves a straightforward means of attack—simply walking into the office and shooting the executive. The attacker did not execute a complicated surveillance or attempt to catch the principal off-guard or away from work. Clearly, not all attacks involve complex logistical planning or surreptitious information gathering.

Potential lessons for an EP specialist include the importance of responding to threats. In this case, the executive had apparently received documented threats. It might have been helpful to report

---

[25] Dawn Walton, "Slain man got threats, police say," *Globe and Mail*, January 18, 2006, p. A10.

those threats to the police and perhaps to have temporarily hired a guard or even someone with EP training. If anyone at the company had spotted a trend in threatening communications or behavior, one useful response might have been to set up a small safe room in a closet or restroom in the office. A panic button at the desk of the receptionist might have warned the principal that a problem person had entered the area. In hindsight, of course, one can recommend many protective measures that might have prevented the attack. These recommendations are not meant to suggest that the murder is the fault of anyone but the murderer. However, executives should be aware that shootings like this one occur all the time. A person in a top position of authority in a business that must deal with irate, violent customers should at least have some means of knowing who is coming to his or her office (perhaps via an access control system or closed-circuit television), as well as a locking, metal door at the entrance to the executive's private office.

Workplace Homicide	
Year	Homicides
1992	1,004
1993	1,074
1994	1,080
1995	1,036
1996	927
1997	860
1998	714
1999	651
2000	677
2001	643(n)
2002	609
2003	632
2004	551

n : Excludes Sept. 11, 2001, terrorist attacks

Source: Bureau of Labor Statistics, Census of Fatal Occupational Injuries, Category: Homicides

A small organization may not have a security department or EP staff to help in such matters. In that case, it may be helpful to seek outside help in conducting a risk assessment and developing some security precautions.

Clearly, workplace homicides in the United States are on the decline. However, the number of such crimes is still significant, and multiple-victim workplace shootings continue to make headlines regularly.

Kidnapping

Kidnapping for ransom is one of the most dangerous threats that principals—and their loved ones and business associates—could face. Kidnappings are aggressive, brutal crimes that are given a great deal of thought by their perpetrators and are sometimes attempted despite the presence of armed security. An analysis of kidnappings of businesspeople in the United States reveals the following general operational patterns:

- In 40 percent of the cases, the kidnappers launched their operations as the intended victims left their residences.

- In 30 percent of the cases, the kidnappers took action once their victims were inside their places of residence (permanent or temporary).

- In 20 percent of the cases, the victim was kidnapped while entering or leaving a vehicle in a residential or office garage or parking lot.

- Creating an automobile accident was the technique of choice in 10 percent of the cases.

Figures on kidnapping are difficult to obtain, but typically 200-300 kidnappings take place in the United States each year. According to an FBI source, about 25 percent are child abductions, and about 50 percent are incidents in which a boyfriend kidnapped a girlfriend or an ex-husband kidnapped an ex-wife. The rest (roughly 50-75 incidents per year) are kidnappings for ransom. In 2000, five executive-level employees were kidnapped. All of them were kidnapped by former employees or known associates and held for ransom. In the United States, kidnapping of executives is not common, but it happens. News of such crimes does not always make national headlines, but EP experts who track executive kidnappings know that enough of them occur to make it essential to work to prevent them. Fortunately, in the United States, kidnapping for ransom may become a less attractive criminal opportunity over time because law enforcement technology is making it increasingly difficult for kidnappers to collect their ransom successfully.

The rate of kidnapping is much higher outside the United States, especially in Latin America and the Middle East. As U.S. businesses expand their operations into Latin America especially, EP specialists should advise protectees of the dangers they may face there.

The following article highlights the dangers in Mexico:[26]

> Although most [kidnapping] victims [in Mexico] aren't killed, authorities warn that amateur kidnappers are fueling the crime wave and that they are more likely to panic and kill their victims even after ransom has been paid….
>
> Here in the Mexican capital, even relatively poor people are abducted and forced to take money out of ATMs. These "express" kidnappings often yield only a few hundred dollars. Some victims are snatched after boarding privately owned "street" taxis.
>
> In the countryside, successful ranchers, store owners and restaurateurs—and their wives and children—are targeted because they are seen as having ready cash. In Acapulco, an American running a successful real estate agency was held for months before ransom was paid.
>
> Police and former police are often involved in the crimes….
>
> Officially in Mexico, there are about 300 kidnappings per year, but security experts say most kidnappings go unreported because police aren't trusted. The real number of abductions is probably several times higher.

The author recently conducted several executive protection training programs in Mexico City. The security professionals with whom he worked, in both the private and government sectors, are striving hard to combat the scourge of kidnapping. The Mexico City metropolitan area has some 20 million residents,

---

[26] Laurence Iliff, *Dallas Morning News*, January 24, 2005.

significant traffic congestion, a high crime rate, and other factors that pose serious EP challenges. An EP specialist charged with protecting a principal on a trip to Mexico City should link up with a local company that has a proven track record, knows the city, and understands the proper approach to executive protection.

One source, the consulting group Control Risks, names the following countries as the top 10 for kidnapping in 2005:

1. Mexico
2. Colombia
3. Brazil
4. Haiti
5. Iraq
6. Venezuela
7. India
8. Trinidad and Tobago
9. Bangladesh
10. Argentina

The introduction to this book describes in some detail the kidnapping of businessman Edward Lampert. The next case study describes a close call by a family member of a different businessman.

Attempt Against a Principal's Son

In November 2004, a cocaine addict who used to manage the personal financial portfolio of New Jersey real estate magnate James M. Weichert pleaded guilty to hatching a plot to kidnap Mr. Weichert's 21-year-old son.[27]

Needy for money, former investment broker Robert E. Harrison conceived a plan to kidnap Weichert's son for ransom,

---

[27] Details compiled from several news accounts, including "Ex-Broker Admits Plot to Kidnap Weichert Heir," www.wnbc.com, November 19, 2004.

bought duct tape and a BB gun, and made a call on August 10 to try to meet with the intended victim. Authorities found an unsigned ransom note that said "we" had researched Weichert's significant assets but would demand a modest $1 million in cash. "What we absolutely demand is payment in the next 60 minutes," the note said. "This can be simple and cheap or personally devastating. We are civilized people. If you comply, this will be over quickly. If you choose to play games the only possible outcome is very unpleasant. Consider what would be lost if you make a mistake."

Morris County, New Jersey, prosecutors said Harrison called the 21-year-old and pretended to be a Detective Chris Stone of the New Vernon Police Department. Harrison told the son that he found paperwork belonging to him in a Mercedes-Benz that was abandoned in a cemetery in Harding, New Jersey, and that he needed him to come to the cemetery to look over the documents. Fortunately, the son was suspicious and notified his father, who called police. There is no New Vernon Police Department; New Vernon is a section of Harding. The call to the son was traced back to Harrison's cellular telephone.

Harrison had been Mr. Weichert's stockbroker at Merrill Lynch, but Weichert was unhappy with the quality of his work and refused to use him after October 2000.

Lessons Learned. In a sense, when kidnappers grab an executive, they are taking the wrong person. Kidnapping the wealthy head of a business ties up the very person most able to make decisions and obtain large amounts of money. Although kidnappers most often take the principal himself or herself, kidnapping the spouse or a child makes more sense. EP specialists should realize that, at least in a traditional kidnapping for ransom, a principal's family members may be attractive targets: they tend to be surrounded with little or no security, and taking them leaves the principal free to obtain the ransom money.

The Weichert case also shows the value of security awareness. The sense that something is not quite right can be invaluable. EP specialists should make a point of providing principals and their families with periodic security awareness briefings in order to help them avoid attacks.

Kidnapping Summaries

This section provides brief accounts of a number of abductions of businesspeople around the world. Lessons learned are presented after the group of summaries.

Canadian Kidnapped in Haiti[28]

> A Montreal businesswoman who lives in Haiti was kidnapped from her home in Port-au-Prince over the weekend....
>
> Family members, who live in Montreal, say her captors are demanding a $300,000 US ransom. Her husband fears her life is in danger.
>
> She is a Canadian citizen of Haitian origin who runs a phone card business, and is based in Port-au-Prince, Haiti.
>
> Reports say she was in her home when her kidnappers broke in and took her away.

Approximately four days later, the businesswoman was released after ransom was paid.

Daughter of Ex-President Kidnapped and Killed[29]

> The daughter of former Paraguayan President Raul Cubas was found dead Wednesday night, months after she was abducted in the highest-profile kidnapping in this South American country....
>
> Cecilia Cubas was seized by heavily armed gunmen in a commando-style operation Sept. 21 as she drove near the family home in Asuncion.

---

[28] "Montrealer kidnapped in Haiti," CBC News, June 14, 2005, www.cbc.ca/montreal/story/qc-kidnap20050613.html.

[29] "Daughter of ex-Paraguayan president found dead," February 16, 2005, MSNBC on-line, www.msnbc.msn.com/id/6983329/.

Other sources report that an $800,000 ransom was paid—obviously in vain—for the release of the 32-year-old woman.

Business Heir Kidnapped in Sweden[30]

A 24-year-old man has been arrested in Denmark suspected of kidnapping a Swedish millionaire businessman, who was found alive earlier this month after two weeks in captivity....

The suspect...is the third man arrested in the case.... The man was transferred to Sweden today.

Fabian Bengtsson, 32, was abducted on January 17 [2005] in Gothenburg [Sweden] on his way to work at Siba, a family-owned nationwide home electronics retail chain of which he is managing director and which he will one day inherit.

He was not released until February 3, when he was found in a Gothenburg city park.

Police have said that while a ransom was demanded for his release, no money was ever paid out.

A first suspect, a 43-year-old Croatian man, was arrested on February 10 at his home in Gothenburg on the basis of information Bengtsson was able to provide to police.

He has admitted to kidnapping Bengtsson, saying through his lawyer that his motive was money.

Another man was arrested in Vienna last week in connection with the case. According to press reports, the man is a Swede who reportedly masterminded the kidnapping but did not take part in it. He is expected to be transferred from Austria to Sweden soon....

Fabian Bengtsson's personal fortune has been estimated at between six and 16 million kronor [$800,000 to $2 million].

Business Owner Kidnapped and Killed in Dallas[31]

Dallas restaurateur Oscar Sanchez was shot as he was trying to escape hours after kidnappers snatched him from an Oak

---

[30] "Third suspect arrested in kidnapping," *Herald Sun* on-line, www.heraldsun.news.com.au.

[31] Jason Trahan, Scott Parks, and Ernesto Londoño, "Police find body of missing restaurateur," *Dallas Morning News*, January 28, 2005.

Cliff street 10 days ago, police told his family Thursday.

The grim news came as searchers found Mr. Sanchez's body in a cold, rain-soaked field in South Dallas. His remains were covered with construction debris.

"From what we know, it appears that Oscar was killed only a few hours after his abduction...in an attempt to escape his captors," said Mike McKinley, attorney for the Sanchez family....

The discovery of Mr. Sanchez's remains solved the mystery of his whereabouts but shed no light on why he was targeted for kidnapping. His family and their spokesman said it was all about money.

[One suspect] had been a waiter at the popular El Ranchito restaurant on Jefferson Boulevard in Oak Cliff. Mr. Sanchez and his family own the restaurant and often held business meetings there. The family also owns La Calle Doce restaurants in Oak Cliff and Lakewood.

"Since many of these meetings were held over lunch or dinner at the restaurant, the family believes it is likely that [the suspect who worked there] and/or others may have overheard parts of these conversations and, together with the fact that the Sanchez family operated a successful and high-profile business for a number of years, derived at their conclusion that they could extort money from the family by kidnapping a family member" Mr. McKinley said....

[Another suspect] owns the Duncanville home where Mr. Sanchez was shot and killed. Earlier that day, Mr. Sanchez had been abducted when a white sedan rammed the back of his black Honda Civic a few blocks from his Oak Cliff home. The incident appeared to be a staged fender-bender, police said.

Mr. McKinley said it appeared that the kidnappers had been keeping Mr. Sanchez under surveillance for several weeks before the kidnapping.... Kidnappers contacted the family repeatedly with ransom demands on the day of the abduction. Police said the kidnappers first wanted $3 million but gradually dropped their demand to $78,000 when the family insisted they could only come up with that much cash.

The family and the kidnappers arranged for the money to be dropped in Arlington, but no one showed up to claim the cash, police said.

Lessons Learned. It is not necessary to be genuinely wealthy in order to be a kidnapping target—only to be relatively wealthy or to seem to have some access to money. Kidnappers in Mexico target people of modest means, for example, and several of the preceding kidnapping summaries involve victims whose families are well-to-do but not in the *Forbes* 500 range.

A particular challenge for the EP specialist is protecting a principal in a country where police may be in league with kidnappers. When employing local security assistance, it is essential to make sure the provider is not in the kidnapping business. The EP specialist may be able to find a trusted supplier of security services by consulting EP colleagues in other companies who have successfully worked with the supplier in the past.

As in the Sanchez case, when a businessperson is kidnapped, it is not unusual to learn later that an employee was part of the plot.

Kidnappers often use the technique of forcing an automobile crash. Executives may be well advised to take security driving training (which may help the executive escape the situation) and to use protected vehicles, which aid escape with their sturdy construction, powerful engines, run-flat tires, and bullet-resistant windows and metal panels.

Kidnapping Recommendations

The ordinary activities of executive protection involve moving the principal safely from point to point and keeping him or her secure at home, at work, and anywhere else the principal may go. Those activities protect the executive not just from kidnapping but from a wide variety of risks.

However, certain additional measures should be taken to reduce the likelihood of kidnapping and to mitigate the harm that would result from such an attack. Kidnapping-specific EP measures include kidnap and ransom (K&R) insurance, tabletop exercises, and collection of key personal information about the principal.

Kidnap and Ransom Insurance

K&R insurance not only assists with ransom payment but also establishes, in advance, an arrangement with a response organization that is experienced in dealing with kidnappings. K&R insurance policies typically include the following clauses: [32]

> **Kidnapping and Extortion Coverage.** Essentially this is for ransom money and payments to prevent such acts as damage to tangible property, the dissemination of proprietary information, or the introduction of a computer virus.

> **Custody Coverage.** This protects against the ransom money disappearing en route to the kidnappers. For example, a courier could be robbed or killed, or the money could be lost in a fire.

> **Expense Coverage.** This includes coverage for a multitude of costs incurred related to victim recovery and rehabilitation. It also covers any necessary independent forensics tests, interest costs for loans that the insured may have to take out, and any reward money paid.

> **Accidental Loss.** This includes accidental death and dismemberment in case victims lose a finger, arm, or their life.

Tabletop Exercises

K&R policies typically include arrangements for crisis assistance. In other words, if a covered executive is kidnapped, a firm that is experienced in dealing with such situations is supposed to provide practical assistance in dealing with police, communicating with the kidnappers, delivering the ransom, and performing other key functions when time is at a premium and the executive's colleagues and family members are upset.

Most companies now have a crisis response team consisting of members of top management and other employees in key departments (such as information technology and personnel). It is prudent to have the crisis team hold a tabletop exercise annually to test the kidnapping response capability of the company, the K&R insurance provider, and the designated response organization.

---

[32] "Watch Your Back," *Bloomberg Wealth Manager*, February 2004, p. 31.

The exercise should address kidnapping both in the United States and overseas. The plan should include a decision tree, contact lists, resource lists, and other details. It should also include training for the principals regarding security awareness, code words, and kidnapping survival.

In a crisis, especially a kidnap or hostage situation, there is no time to waste, and it is better to have made many important decisions and gathered key information in advance, during calmer moments.

An even more advanced level of preparation involves conducting a tabletop exercise in the country in which the principal will be doing business. The author conducted a tabletop exercise in Mexico City for a *Fortune* 50 company (U.S.-based, as all companies on that list are). Being in the city and dealing with local contacts added to the realism of the exercise. That approach helps the EP team practice dealing with such factors as language barriers, unfamiliar laws and legal systems, and different cultures.

Key Personal Information

In case a principal should go missing for any reason, it would be helpful to have on hand certain personal information that would aid in the search. The information should be gathered and kept sealed and secure, to be opened only in an emergency. The following are recommended elements to include in the emergency information packet:

Name

Title

Office location

Photos of principal, spouse, and children (digital for ease of sharing)

Completed DNA kit (see details in Chapter 7: Technology)

Physical description

Scars or identifying marks

Digital video (with sound) capturing principal's appearance, voice, mannerisms, etc.

Date and place of birth

Residence address and phone number

Secondary residence address and phone number

Special medication requirements and drug allergies

Locations, contact names, phone numbers, and schedules for regular events (e.g., children's schools, teachers, and principals)

Copy of driver's license and passport.

Doctor, dentist, and pharmacy names, addresses, and phone numbers

Blood type

Driver's license (state, county, number, expiration date)

Passport (country, number, expiration date)

Similar information about spouse

Household staff (position, name, address, phone number, passport number, nationality, driver's license number)

Personally owned vehicles (make/type, year, color, state, registered owner, license number, insurance carrier, policy number)

Car phone numbers

Emergency phrase that only the principal knows (EP staff will see it if the emergency information packet needs to be opened)—to prove that the principal is who he or she claims to be and is in jeopardy

Other Attacks

Executives and wealthy persons may be attacked not just by terminated employees, disgruntled customers, protesters, street criminals, and terrorists. Risk also comes from unexpected sources, particularly the insider threat:

As case in point is that of Edmond Safra, a 67-year-old billionaire banker of Lebanese descent. Mr. Safra died of suffocation in a fire within his residence in Monte Carlo, Monaco, on December 4, 1999. The fire was set by a trusted employee who worked as one of Mr. Safra's nurses within the residence.[33]

The nurse had a strong desire for the principal's attention, and he also had a conflict with the head nurse. Mr. Safra's security personnel were posted at a nearby villa, but no EP staff members were with the principal at the time of the attack. Once the fire was discovered, Mr. Safra's chief of security rushed to the apartment, but because he had no ID or keys, police blocked his entrance and he was unable to help his employer.

Lessons Learned. First, EP specialists should be aware that an attack against a principal may come not from someone who hates the principal but from someone who is dearly attached to the principal. Second, it is vital to have some way in which a principal can quickly summon help from protective staff. Third, EP staff should have a means of entering the principal's living quarters in case of an emergency. Fourth, part of an EP specialist's job is to expect the unexpected—that is, to think about potential risks and then devise preventive measures to keep them from occurring.

---

[33] Details compiled from various news sources, including Karl Taro Greenfeld, "Murder by Fire," *Time*, December 13, 1999.

5.
Countersurveillance

What, Why, and When

Adversaries who wish to attack a principal almost always conduct surveillance to learn about the principal's appearance, commuting routes, travel practices, residential and office security measures, and executive protection detail. Case studies make it crystal clear that adversaries watch before they strike. Now, many private and government EP details are using *countersurveillance* to watch the watchers. For example, at an event at which the principal will be speaking, the main EP detail may stand near the principal in order to protect him or her, but a member of the EP team may be assigned to blend into—and conduct countersurveillance on—the audience. The EP specialist conducting countersurveillance looks carefully and subtly to see whether anyone is photographing the security operation, taking notes on protective measures, touching what might be a concealed weapon, or exhibiting signs of stress that could be related to an impending attack. Watchers sometimes watch their targets so closely that they can be detected and their plans deflected.

A related method of addressing surveillance by adversaries is *antisurveillance*. Thus, this chapter examines three types of watching:

- Surveillance: the practice of observing a target (in this case, the principal) to gain information on it
- Countersurveillance: measures taken by individuals or groups under surveillance to monitor the activities of persons who are watching them
- Antisurveillance: procedures to neutralize surveillance that has been detected or is reasonably suspected

Countersurveillance supports executive protection in several important ways. It can help EP specialists detect an act that is in the planning stage, prevent an attack from occurring, and make an attack more difficult to carry out.

In some cases, particularly for principals facing an especially high threat level, EP staff should conduct countersurveillance often or always. In other cases, EP staff may need to conduct countersurveillance only occasionally. However, in those latter cases, EP staff should be attentive to developments that may increase the need for countersurveillance. When and where the threat level is higher (e.g., if an obviously threatening letter has been received or the principal's public profile has suddenly become much higher or more controversial), the EP program may need to regularly plant observers in the crowd or assign them to follow the principal's vehicle at a distance to watch for adversaries who might be observing the principal and his or her protective measures.

The rest of this chapter examines the signs and practices of surveillance (that is, what countersurveillance is looking for), the methods of countersurveillance, and several means of antisurveillance.

Surveillance by Adversaries

Over the years, enough attacks have been launched against principals that EP experts have been able to discern a pattern in the steps of that process. A standard attack methodology is as follows:

1. Target selection
2. Initial surveillance
3. Final target selection
4. Plan (final surveillance)
5. Attack team deployment
6. Target arrival
7. Action

As the list shows, surveillance in one form or another constitutes two of the seven steps in the standard attack methodology. Thus, surveillance by adversaries is a worthy object of an EP specialist's attention. Detecting an adversary's information gathering (through countersurveillance) or interrupting it (through antisurveillance) may cause the adversary to abandon or fail in his or her attempt to harm the principal.

To conduct countersurveillance, one must know what to look for. That requires an understanding of surveillance techniques. When adversaries conduct surveillance of a target, their goal is, in a sense, to gather information that will enable them to assemble the pieces of a puzzle. The following are some of the questions they are attempting to answer through their surveillance efforts:

- **Home.** Where does the principal live? How is the home protected? How does the principal enter and exit the home? How could the adversary enter or damage the home?

- **Office.** Where does the principal work? How is the workplace protected? How does the principal enter and exit the workplace? How could the adversary enter or damage the workplace?

- **Vehicles.** In what vehicles does the principal travel?

Does the principal travel in a convoy? Are the vehicles armored? Does the principal do the driving? Is the principal accompanied by EP staff?

- **Routes and destinations.** By what routes does the principal typically travel? To what destinations other than home or office does the principal frequently go? Are there any vulnerable (that is, attack-friendly or less secure) places to which the principal often goes?

- **Predictability.** When does the principal typically leave the home, arrive at work, go out for lunch, leave the office, and arrive at home?

- **Security detail.** Does the principal's security detail consist of a driver only? Does the driver appear to be trained in security? Does the principal typically use both a driver and an EP specialist? Do they seem alert and ready? What do they look like? Do any EP specialists accompany the principal to meetings or social outings?

Surveillance methods can be divided into three categories—fixed, moving, and technical:

- **Fixed surveillance.** The adversary maintains a position from which he or she can observe the principal's activities or locations associated with the principal (such as the home or office). The adversary also makes every attempt to blend into the local culture in terms of dress, mannerisms, and schedules. Several adversaries may work together to gather more information.

- **Moving surveillance.** The adversary follows the principal on foot or by vehicle, attempting not to be noticed. Again, several adversaries may work together to increase the likelihood of following the principal successfully.

- **Technical surveillance.** The adversary uses technology to record conversations in rooms or automobiles or to capture data from computers, telephones (land-line or mobile), fax machines, and other communications devices.

An additional characteristic of surveillance has to do with the time over which it is conducted. Surveillance may be extended over a long period so the adversary can discern patterns, or it may take place on just a few occasions so the adversary can minimize his or her chances of being detected.

In the past, adversaries have gone to great lengths to conduct surveillance of their targets. Arthur Bremer, the would-be assassin who shot presidential candidate George Wallace in 1972, carefully tracked the movements of President Nixon, his original target. When Yigal Amir assassinated former Prime Minister of Israel Yitzhak Rabin in 1995, he had already planned two other attempts, which fell apart just before they were to be carried out. On the third attempt, Amir detected the location of Rabin's limousine and lurked there until he could complete the assassination.

Those attacks took place some time ago. Do today's adversaries still conduct surveillance to plan their attacks? The answer is an unequivocal yes, as the following account shows:[34]

> An Al Qaeda operative who carefully studied the headquarters building of Prudential Financial, Inc., in Newark, NJ,... photographed the building from a Starbucks coffee house across the street and sent a detailed 40-page surveillance report to his superiors in Pakistan that suggested how Al Qaeda could explode a bomb near or inside the structure and kill hundreds of Prudential employees.... [T]hen-secretary of [the Department of Homeland Security] Tom Ridge announced...that Prudential's headquarters, as well as the headquarters buildings of Citigroup and the New York Stock Exchange in Manhattan and the International Monetary Fund and World Bank in Washington, DC, had all been targeted for terrorist attacks by Al Qaeda.

The suspected terrorist's report about Prudential contained

---

[34] Jacob Goodwin, "Exclusive: Al Qaeda's Plot on Prudential Revealed," *Government Security News*, May 23, 2005, p. 1.

more than 100 photos, some which he took himself on the streets of Newark, others which he had photocopied or scanned from the pages of various freely-available commemorative books about the history of Prudential or from the company's Web site....

The report was chilling [to Prudential's security director] because it described the security precautions in place at Prudential and recommended various ways to defeat those security measures in cold and calculating tones....

[The suspect's report described] the types of ID badges worn by Prudential's employees, the color of the chains that those ID badges are hung on, and the fact that some of the building's exterior surveillance cameras had frosted glass which makes it hard to tell which way those cameras are pointed. The suspected terrorist also suggested that follow-up Al Qaeda surveillance teams should attempt to gather further information by talking to Prudential employees who could be approached while they smoked cigarettes outside the building.

Countersurveillance Methods

This section examines two primary categories of countersurveillance: looking for and tracking, by vehicle and on foot, any adversaries who might be conducting a surveillance of the principal, and carefully investigating any suspicious persons who visit the principal's office, home, or other key location.

Pedestrian and Vehicular Methods

In countersurveillance there is much room for creativity. The EP program may station its own EP specialists in crowds where the principal is speaking, along sidewalks outside the principal's home or office garage, or near the entrance to the principal's workplace. The risk of detection may be reduced by using younger people, who do not obviously appear to be part of the EP team but have been trained in what to look for. If the principal will spend a good deal of time walking through public spaces, such as a convention's exhibit hall, an EP specialist could be assigned to walk some distance behind the principal to detect whether anyone is paying him an undue, suspicious amount or type of attention.

To conduct countersurveillance of a principal's commuting or other regular driving routes, the EP team can use a countersurveillance vehicle of an inconspicuous type, containing inconspicuous occupants, to follow the protection detail along its route, at a distance, to identify possible surveillance. The principal's driver can make a point of driving through natural chokepoints that will show whether an adversary is following the principal or can take a circuitous but realistic route that will force the adversary to double back (which no one but someone conducting surveillance would have cause to do) or to drive close to the countersurveillance vehicle (so its occupants can identify the person or persons conducting the surveillance).

Like surveillance, countersurveillance requires a degree of skill. Those conducting it must take care not to be discovered and must find effective and subtle ways to capture the information they seek. The following is a list of common mistakes made by countersurveillance operatives:

- correlated movement (clearly matching the movement of the countersurveillance target)
- crude or inappropriate disguises
- visible communications equipment
- obvious note taking
- excessive picture taking

In addition to avoiding detection, countersurveillance operatives must develop observation skills beyond those that casual observers employ. To increase their likelihood of capturing useful information, they should do the following:

- Practice being alert and security conscious.
- Favor detailed descriptions over casual observations.
- Practice estimating time, direction, and distance.

- Become familiar with descriptive terms, shades of colors, models of vehicles, etc.
- Practice observing, identifying, and memorizing people's sex, race, height, weight, age, and distinguishing features, such as facial hair, tattoos, glasses, and clothing.

Investigating Visitors of Concern

In many cases, people who are adversaries or will later become adversaries actually visit or attempt to visit the principal or his or her workplace or home. It seems unsubtle for a person with a grudge against a principal to storm into the office building, knock on the door at the principal's home, or approach the principal's executive assistant and ask detailed questions about the principal, but those acts happen often. Such people are called visitors of concern. When they show themselves, they provide EP staff with an excellent opportunity to discover them, research them, and perhaps, by doing so, dissuade them from pursuing their plan of attack.

The EP program should establish several key steps that it will routinely take in response to a visit from a person of concern. Those steps include policy, categorization, interviews, collection of general information, use of appropriate interview techniques, and some administrative procedures to conclude the process.

Policy

As a matter of policy, anyone who appears without an appointment or invitation to seek a visit with a protectee should, to the degree possible, be interviewed to determine whether the person may pose a threat.

Categorization

Uninvited visitors may be categorized as follows:

- **The curious.** These people are interested in prominent figures, such as business executives, celebrities, and politicians. They are easily turned away in their attempts to get close to a principal.

- **The nuisance.** These people are nearly obsessive in making contact via mail or in person. Their interest in a principal is inconvenient and obnoxious, but it rarely develops into an actual threat.

- **The potentially dangerous.** These are people who have made direct or implied threats against the principal.

Interviews

If it is possible to interview the visitor, several key factors come into play: timing, location, and preparation. An EP specialist should arrange to interview the visitor as soon as is practical. If the interview will take place at the principal's place of work, it should be held in an interview room away from the security office. It is even better to conduct the interview at the visitor's home, as the interviewer can observe the visitor's overall lifestyle and see conditions inside the home. That information may lead to insights about the visitor's motivation and level of dangerousness, if any. The EP specialist can conduct a more effective interview if he or she gathers preliminary information about the subject's background and interests beforehand.

Collection of General Information

Through interviews and research, the EP specialist should attempt to gain as much of the following information about the visitor as possible:

- Identifiers
  - name and aliases
  - date of birth
  - social security and military identification numbers
  - current address
  - names and addresses of close relatives

- physical description and current photograph
- handwriting samples
- Background information
  - education and training
  - criminal history
  - history of violent behavior
  - military history
  - expertise in and history of use of weapons
  - employment history
  - mental health history
  - history of grievances
  - history of harassing others
  - travel history, especially in the previous year
- Current life situation and circumstances
  - existence of a stable living situation, including whether basic needs for food, clothing, shelter, and human contact are met
  - employment
  - status of being scheduled for discharge from a hospital, mental institution, or correctional facility
  - appearance of being on a downward course
- Behaviors of concern
  - interest in assassination
  - ideas about and plans for attacking a public figure, official, celebrity, or corporate executive
  - communication of an inappropriate interest in a figure, especially comments that express or imply interest in attacking the person
  - visiting a place associated with a protectee
  - approaching a protectee

Interview Techniques

When interviewing the visitor, the EP specialist should express, in words and manner, a tone or feeling of sympathy and understanding. Such an approach often leads an interview subject to trust the interviewer. The EP specialist should also maintain a patient, professional demeanor, even when presented with ludicrous comments.

In forming questions, it is best to use open-ended questions— that is, ones that cannot readily be answered with a yes or no. Such questions get the interview subject comfortable with talking to the EP specialist and may lead to useful discussion. Of course, some direct, specific questions must be asked about the subject's background, experiences, and life style.

Even if the interview seems to be flowing smoothly, the EP specialist should be alert for evasive answers and signs of anger or anxiety. It is also prudent to avoid extensive note taking or obvious use of recording devices, as such practices may make the subject feel inhibited about speaking.

Administrative Procedures

After the interview, the EP specialist should review the experience and classify the visitor into one of the categories described earlier. If the visitor falls into the category of the curious, there is probably no need for further interviews. If the visitor can be classed as a nuisance, a follow-up interview should be scheduled to gain more information and to convince the person to stay away from the principal. Finally, if the information gathered from the interview and other research suggests that the person may be dangerous, the EP specialist should look into obtaining additional support from local, state, and federal authorities.

Antisurveillance

As was noted at the beginning of this chapter, antisurveillance consists of procedures to neutralize surveillance that has been detected or is reasonably suspected. Three varieties of antisurveillance include operations security (OPSEC), technical surveillance countermeasures (TSCM), and unpredictability.

OPSEC

In executive protection, operations security (OPSEC) refers to the concept of protecting the EP program itself. In other words, the EP program protects the principal, and OPSEC protects the EP program. OPSEC is a form of antisurveillance in that it seeks to deny adversaries the information they seek about the protection effort. The particular approach that OPSEC pursues is to conceal indicators, activities, and data that a smart adversary might be able to piece together to create usable information.

OPSEC is traditionally divided into five stages. The following explanation of those stages is based on a system described in guidelines developed by the American chemical industry shortly after the September 11, 2001, terror attacks against the United States.[35] However, the list has been tailored for use in an EP program. In using OPSEC, EP specialists take the following steps:

1. *Identify critical information.* What would an adversary need to know about the EP program and the principal's office, home, and vehicles in order to launch a successful attack against the principal?

2. *Conduct a threat assessment.* Who has the desire and capability to attack the principal?

3. *Perform a vulnerability analysis.* What are the weak points in the principal's overall armor? How could an adversary enter the home or office or gain access to a vehicle transporting the principal? How could an adversary obtain the information needed to carry out an attack? Could an ad-

---

[35] American Chemistry Council, Chlorine Institute, and Synthetic Organic Chemical Manufacturers Association, *Site Security Guidelines for the U.S. Chemical Industry* (Arlington, VA: ACC, 2001).

versary develop the necessary information by combining small, seemingly insignificant data that is publicly available? Do the company's Web sites, government-required filings, and annual reports divulge more information than is necessary?

4. *Assess the risk.* Weighing the threat (the level of the adversary's desire and abilities) and vulnerability (weak points in defenses), what is the probability that the adversary will succeed in an attack? What would be the effect of the adversary's success?

5. *Apply countermeasures.* What means of protecting spoken information, documents, computers, and networks would keep the adversary from obtaining the needed information?

Countermeasures for protecting conversations and hard-copy documents include the following:

- relying on face-to-face conversations for discussions of the most sensitive information
- using encryption for cell phone and radio communications
- avoiding conversations in public areas (such as lobbies, restaurants, or airports)
- applying "need-to-know" procedures for sharing information within the EP program or the company
- instituting a clean desk policy
- shredding documents
- appropriately securing documents by locking offices, file cabinets, and trash bins
- including information protection clauses in contracts for outside services
- training and reminding employees about document security techniques

Additional countermeasures may be needed to protect information that is stored in electronic format on computers and networks. The EP program should do (or have other departments in the company do) the following:[36]

- Physically secure computer rooms and telecommunications rooms with electronic access control systems that record ingress and egress.

- Employ firewalls, virus protection, encryption, user identification, and message and user authentication to protect both the main computer network and any subsidiary networks, such as access control systems, that are connected to it or to the outside.

- Teach employees to beware of ruses to obtain their computer passwords (also called human engineering).

- Set a user's level of data access based on the principles of "least access," "separation of functions," and "need to know," not on precedent or a person's position.

- Remove any signs indicating the location of the main computer room.

- Allow only authorized personnel to enter central computer rooms. Supervise any visitors.

- Do not give keys or lock combinations to visitors.

- Require employees to notify management in advance if they wish to enter the computer room during hours when they are not scheduled to be working.

TSCM

The term technical surveillance refers to surveillance that employs electronic eavesdropping devices, and countermeasures are the steps one takes to stop such eavesdropping—hence the term technical surveillance countermeasures. TSCM is thus clearly a

---

[36] Adapted from *Site Security Guidelines for the U.S. Chemical Industry*.

form of antisurveillance, as it is designed very directly to stop adversaries form gathering information about the principal and his or her activities and security measures.

As a surveillance technique, electronic eavesdropping is now within reach of anyone, not just those who are government-trained in the art of espionage. Miniature audio and video devices that require little power and can transmit their signals to the eavesdropper are inexpensive and readily available through catalogs, the Internet, and stores. At least at the lower end of sophistication, electronic eavesdropping is clearly a simple, do-it-yourself project.

By contrast, TSCM is not a technique that the EP program can carry out in-house. It is a narrow specialty that requires technical training and expensive equipment. If EP staff have reason to suspect that the principal may be the target of electronic surveillance, or if the overall threat level seems high enough to warrant extra measures, the EP program should turn to a reputable TSCM firm to examine, or sweep, the principal's office, conference rooms, and possibly even home.

Because TSCM technicians are not qualified by a central authority, it can be difficult to select a firm confidently. It may help to consult local law enforcement for recommendations. The regional office of the FBI may also be able to offer advice. Some EP specialists feel most confident when they select TSCM technicians who have been trained in the federal government (in military or civilian agencies).

Beyond the challenge of selecting a firm, there is the matter of cost. TSCM is expensive. It is common for a TSCM sweep to cost several hundred dollars per hour. However, in searching for resources to cover that expense, the EP team should point out to corporate finance officers that TSCM is also a valuable tool for preventing theft of trade secrets. In fact, it is probably used much more for that purpose than for executive protection.

What is it like to work with a TSCM firm? One expert describes the experience as follows:[37]

> Here's a sample of what to expect from a person who has had the education, training, and experience to be able to offer a quality counterespionage TSCM sweep. He might have you take a drive along a city street that you rarely use. You may stop at a pay phone you've never used before. You would never use any telephone billed in your name or in your company's name to discuss The Problem with him or his firm. On the job, you would continue to behave and talk as you previously did. You would tell no one except your corporate security manager about your request for TSCM. The team would arrive unannounced, to be escorted by the corporate security manager to the target area. They would remain therein undisturbed until they tell you otherwise.

The reason for keeping the search a secret is that if the eavesdropper learned of an impending sweep, he or she might turn off or remove any listening devices that had been planted. If turned off, they are more difficult to find. If removed, they are of course impossible to find and may be put back in place after the sweep.

The TSCM sweep itself employs both physical and electronic searches. In the physical search, the TSCM team (usually two or three people) examines the following:

- walls
- drop ceilings
- raised floors (such as in computer rooms)
- furniture
- cable and wire conduits and closets
- heating and air conditioning ducts
- computers, fax machines, and telephones, along with their power and communications connections

In its electronic search, the team uses specialized equipment to discover electronic eavesdropping devices. Common

---

[37] Peter Pitorri, *Counterespionage for American Business* (Woburn, MA: Butterworth-Heinemann, 1998).

TSCM equipment includes the following:

- scanning countermeasures receiver
- spectrum analyzer
- communications receiver
- nonlinear junction detector
- differential radio-frequency detector
- telephone and telephone line tester
- cable checker
- thermal imaging device
- X-ray machine

After the physical and electronic searches, TSCM technicians will inform the EP staff of any eavesdropping devices found. They should also make recommendations regarding the best ways to prevent future eavesdropping. For example, if a telephone wire lies too near a computer, it may serve as an antenna for an eavesdropping device.

Unpredictability

An effective way to frustrate an adversary is to make the principal's movements and protective measures unpredictable. Unpredictability makes surveillance difficult, forces adversaries to risk increased exposure to gather the information they desire, increases the challenge of planning an attack, and makes execution of an attack much more difficult.

The goal is to create uncertainty in the adversary's mind. This can be done by changing the principal's routes (in vehicles and on foot), alternating times of departure from home or work, rotating the vehicles used, occasionally using vehicles not associated with the protectee at all, sending out occasional decoy details (without the protectee), varying the number of people in the protective detail, varying the number of vehicles used in the detail, and varying the configuration of the detail.

In sum, watching the watchers and keeping them from gaining the information they need to plan and launch an attack against the principal requires forethought, attention to detail, and a certain degree of guile.

6.
It's Not About the Gun

The famed cyclist Lance Armstrong wrote a memoir called *It's Not About the Bike.* What wins the race, he writes, is not the equipment but the training, perseverance, and brain power of the rider. Likewise, in executive protection, it is not the equipment that preserves the principal's life but the training, perseverance, and brain power of the EP specialist.

In many protective details, firearms are essential tools. However, they must be looked on as the last-ditch response—and one that the EP specialist may have no time to implement. In a given protective setting, guns may or may not be necessary, but they are surely not sufficient. This chapter examines the challenges of EP firearms use, legal and training considerations, complications (and solutions) related to the need for firearms while traveling, and step-down or less-lethal weapons.

Clearly, it is no problem for adversaries anywhere to obtain firearms. In fact, there is a good chance that an adversary or a member of his or her household already owns one. The following are some statistics on U.S. gun ownership:[38]

- There are more than 200 million privately owned firearms in the United States. Of those, at least 65-70 million are handguns. The number rises by approximately 4.5 million annually.

- There are 65-80 million gun owners in the United States. Approximately 30-35 million of them own handguns.

- Roughly 45 percent of American households contain firearms.

The ready availability of firearms to others is one of the reasons EP specialists may wish to carry firearms themselves. Clearly, firearms can serve a worthy purpose in executive protection. For example, in a "cover and evacuate" scenario, it may be critical to return fire. The potential problem lies in thinking that a firearm will get the EP specialist and principal out of trouble every time. In most cases, the EP specialist will never have a chance to pull his or her gun from its holster in time to make a difference. The adversary chooses the time, place, and method of attack, and he or she shows up "gun ready," perhaps with a handgun under a coat or in a large pocket, with a finger on the trigger. By contrast, it is a rare situation in which an EP specialist could walk around "gun ready."

This chapter is not anti-gun. As a law enforcement officer, the author carried a firearm both on-duty and off-duty for 20 years and understands its application. Rather, the chapter attempts to keep the EP value of firearms in perspective. A firearm may help in a desperate situation, but the EP specialist's job is to keep the principal out of desperate situations. EP is not about the gun.

---

[38] National Rifle Association, *2006 Firearms Fact Card*, http://www.nraila.org/Issues/FactSheets/ Read.aspx?ID=83.

Limitations

It is difficult to think of even a single assassination attempt that was stopped by return gunfire from protection officers. Events simply happen too quickly to respond.

For example, the U.S. Secret Service, with all its training and resources, has generally not returned fire at attempted assassins. For example, when John Hinckley, Jr., shot President Reagan in 1981, Secret Service agents could have returned fire but instead focused on covering the President and evacuating him from the scene as quickly as possible.

The Oatman School of Executive Protection has repeatedly demonstrated the strengths and limitations of a firearm response. Using "attack on the principal" (AOP) drills (high-pressure scenarios using real firearms with marking cartridges), participants have learned that firearms, though useful, cannot be the primary means of protecting a principal. In the training scenarios, a student plays the role of an EP specialist who is accompanying a principal in a vehicle driven by a security driver. The vehicle travels to a designated spot, where a confrontation takes place and the student must protect the principal. The student has one firearm and the adversary has one firearm. Eighty percent of the time the adversary wins because he is gun ready. It almost always pays to move the principal out of the situation as quickly as possible instead of standing one's ground and shooting at the adversary. In EP, the first choice is to avoid trouble; the second, to flee from it; and the third, to fight it. If EP specialists have to reach for their guns, they have already failed.

When an attack begins, it is essential to be able to execute a particular series of steps quickly. Those steps have short, memorizable names: *arm's reach*, *sound off*, *cover*, and *evacuate*. The following is what unfolds when, for example, a man draws a handgun and points it at the principal. *Arm's reach* defines the EP specialist's first reaction. If the attacker is within an arm's reach of the agent, the agent should move to immobilize him. If the attacker is beyond an arm's reach of the agent, the agent should move to cover the principal. However, if several agents are guarding the principal, one would grab the principal and others would disarm the attacker.

The second step, *sound off*, means shouting out "Gun!" or "Gun to the right!" or something similar. The message should state the type of weapon and the direction, in relation to the protectee, from which it is coming. Sounding off tells other agents to spring into action and attempts to involve other people in the situation.

Cover means that the agent covers the principal's body with his own. *Evacuate* refers to the overriding need to get the principal out of danger. Stopping to fight an adversary when it would be quicker to dash out a side door is ineffective and dangerous. In most cases, the protective detail should concentrate on shielding and removing the principal, leaving apprehension of the attacker to the police.

Of course, the *arm's reach–sound off–cover–evacuate* response may not be the plan if the protective detail finds itself in the midst of the war on terror in Afghanistan or Iraq. There, a protective detail often has one member who is gun ready, with a finger indexed along the trigger guard, ready to engage the enemy. That is not the normal situation in corporate executive protection, but as businesspeople travel to the world's most dangerous places, such situations can occur. Even then, it is essential for a member of the team to be adept at sensing danger and telling the detail when to remove the principal from a threat.

Permits

A separate challenge in relying too heavily on firearms comes from the multiplicity of laws governing the carrying of concealed weapons. The laws vary from state to state and from site to site, and federal laws sometimes supersede state and local laws and sometimes do not. Even in a state in which the EP specialist is permitted to carry a concealed firearm, there are various locations to which he or she many not bring the gun: schools, airports, churches, some workplaces, certain parks, even restaurants. If the principal suddenly decides to enter a place where the EP specialist cannot bring a gun, two problems arise: (1) what to do with the gun, and (2) how to protect the principal if the EP specialist has come to rely on being armed.

In a major metropolitan area, the variation in gun laws can create a significant challenge even for a short drive. For example, a carry permit in Virginia is not recognized in Maryland, and no private citizen may own, much less carry concealed, a handgun in Washington, DC. Thus, an EP specialist who works mainly in the Virginia suburbs of Washington and needs to meet a principal at Baltimore-Washington Airport in Maryland would have to disarm himself or herself before meeting the principal. Perhaps the EP specialist might lock the unloaded firearm in a gun box in his vehicle and then be able meet the principal. But if the principal then wanted to make a stop in Washington, the EP specialist could not take the principal there unless he or she first disposed of the locked-up, unloaded gun. The laws are so complicated, and interpretations so murky, that carrying a concealed weapon is a distinct challenge for an EP specialist. Moreover, an EP specialist should never try to skirt gun laws, as a violation could land the EP specialist in serious trouble and reflect badly on the principal.

There is one simplifying law, though it applies only to active and retired law enforcement officers—and even then, not to all of them. (There is no national concealed-carry permit for civilians.) On July 22, 2004, President George W. Bush signed H.R. 218, the Law Enforcement Officers' Safety Act, into law. The act, now Public Law 108-277, went into effect immediately. The law exempts qualified active and retired law enforcement officers from local and state prohibitions on the carrying of concealed firearms.

The Fraternal Order of Police produced a white paper explaining the details of the law. Key questions and answers from the paper are given below:[39]

> **Who is eligible to carry concealed firearms under this legislation?**
>
> Qualified law enforcement officers employed by or retired from a local, State or Federal law enforcement agency.
>
> A "qualified active law enforcement officer" is defined as an employee of a government agency who:
>
> - is authorized by law to engage in or supervise the prevention, detection, investigation, prosecution or the incarceration of any person for any violation of law;
>
> - has statutory powers of arrest;
>
> - is authorized by the agency to carry a firearm;
>
> - is not the subject of any disciplinary action by the agency;
>
> - meets the standards, if any, established by the agency which require the employee to regularly qualify in the use of a firearm;
>
> - is not under the influence of alcohol or another intoxicating or hallucinatory drug or substance; and
>
> - is not prohibited by Federal law from possessing a firearm.
>
> Qualified active law enforcement officers must carry the photographic identification issued by the agency for which they are employed.
>
> If you are an active duty law enforcement officer with any local, State or Federal governmental agency and you meet all of the requirements above, you may carry a concealed firearm under the provisions set out in the law.
>
> A "qualified retired law enforcement officer" is defined as an individual who:

---

[39] Fraternal Order of Police, *H.R. 218, the Law Enforcement Officers' Safety Act*, www.grandlodgefop.org/legislation/issues/hr218faq.pdf.

- has retired in good standing from service with a government agency as a law enforcement officer for an aggregate of fifteen (15) years or more for reasons other than mental instability, or retired from such an agency due to a service-connected disability after completing any applicable probationary period of such service;

- was authorized by law to engage in or supervise the prevention, detection, investigation, prosecution or the incarceration of any person for any violation of law;

- had statutory powers of arrest;

- has a nonforfeitable right to benefits under the retirement plan of the agency for which he was employed;

- meets, at his own expense, the same standards for qualification with a firearm as an active officer within the State in which he resides;

- is not under the influence of alcohol or another intoxicating or hallucinatory drug or substance; and

- is not prohibited by Federal law from possessing a firearm.

Qualified retired law enforcement officers must carry the photographic identification issued by the agency for which they were employed and documentation which certifies that they have met, within the most recent twelve month period, the active duty law enforcement standards for qualification for a firearm of the same type as the one they intend to carry. This document must be issued by the retired officer's former agency or from the State in which he lives.

Is the exemption provided by the law total—can I now carry anywhere at any time?

The new law exempts all qualified active and retired law enforcement officers from State and local laws with respect to the carrying of concealed firearms. These officers are not exempt from Federal law or regulation, which governs the carriage of firearms onto aircraft, Federal buildings, Federal property, and national parks.

In addition, State (not local) laws which prohibit the carriage of firearms onto State or local government property and State (not local) laws which allow private entities to prohibit firearms on their private property would still apply to qualified active and retired law enforcement officers.

The Law Enforcement Officers' Safety Act presents a useful benefit to current and retired law enforcement officers who are active in executive protection. The author has taken the mandatory training and is eligible to carry throughout the United States. He has now requalified for the second time under the same standards as active duty police officers in his former department. There is a complete continuity of training. As an EP specialist, he carries the same weapon that he originally qualified with, using the same ammunition that the department uses.

Training

Firearms skill is perishable. If not kept fresh, it will go bad. Therefore, armed EP specialists must train over and over so they can respond correctly in a crisis. Firearms training and proficiency are important not only for the task of EP but also from a liability standpoint. To be on the safe side, it is wise for an EP specialist to qualify with his or her weapon at least twice a year. It is important to keep good records in order to be able to prove that the EP specialist kept up with his or her training.

Armed EP specialists must master three exercises before using a firearm in a protective detail. They must practice and demonstrate the ability to

- holster and re-holster the firearm,
- load and reload the firearm, and
- perform malfunction drills.

These three basic skills must become reflexive behavior or the EP specialist will be doing a disservice to himself or herself and the protectee.

Basic target practice is of some use, but it is even better to practice shooting in all types of conditions: indoors and outdoors, in daylight and at night, in dry weather and wet, in hot and cold temperatures, at medium distances and in close quarters. In addition, it is extremely valuable to engage in scenario training in which the EP specialist makes shoot/don't shoot decisions and practices returning fire. Moreover, it makes sense to train with the weapon that will be used on the job—and also in the type of clothes that will be worn on the job. It takes some practice to move one's tie, suit coat, and overcoat out of the way to reach a firearm quickly.

The choice of ammunition also requires careful consideration. EP is close work, and one does not want a high-powered round to hit the adversary and then keep going. The firearm and ammunition must be matched correctly for the task. Law enforcement agencies select firearms and ammunition to meet the daily danger on the streets. Thus, if an EP specialist plans to carry a firearm, it can be instructive to find out what the local police are carrying.

All EP specialists, armed or not, must be "switched on" (that is, alert and keenly attentive) whenever they are on protective duty. Armed EP specialists will need special training to be able to pull their weapons from their holsters quickly and return fire while primarily working to remove their principals from harm's way. It is a lot to do all at once, so frequent training is essential.

Detecting Armed Adversaries

This section discusses ways in which an EP specialist can detect armed adversaries. First, though, it is important to clarify that if an EP specialist does detect someone who he or she suspects may be carrying a concealed firearm, it is time to move the principal away from the possibly armed person. To do so might even require leaving the event. If the person begins to follow the principal and protective detail, the EP team will have to make some important decisions. That stage of EP, however, is not the subject of this section.

In trying to detect armed adversaries, two key questions arise:

(1) how to tell whether a person is carrying a concealed firearm, and (2) how to tell whether an armed person is a friend (such as an off-duty police officer) or foe.

To answer the first question, an EP specialist can be trained to look for numerous visual cues—the tell-tale signs. Observation skills go a long way in executive protection.

When someone carries a concealed firearm, the weapon usually leaves an imprint of some sort. If the EP specialist looks closely enough, he or she may be able to spot the weapon's outline even under clothing. Another identifier is weight and symmetry. If someone is concealing a gun in a jacket that he or she is wearing, the weight of the gun makes the jacket look off kilter, as one side will be heavier than the other. When the person walks or runs, the side of the jacket that contains the gun will swing differently than the empty side. Another clothing-based clue is the choice of garments. A person wishing to conceal a weapon may dress more warmly than the weather warrants—for example, wearing a coat, jacket, or heavy shirt on a hot day to hide the weapon.

A different set of clues comes from body language. People who carry a concealed firearm (whether legally or illegally) have a tendency to conduct a security check on the firearm, meaning they periodically place a hand where the gun is to make sure it is still in place. For example, when getting up from a table or climbing out of a car, an armed person will generally pat or adjust the place where he or she is carrying the gun (such as the right hip or the inside breast pocket of a jacket). When the person walks, his or her arm on the side where the gun is stored will have a tendency to stay in place, not swing like the other arm. Especially when the person runs, he or she will reach for the weapon where it is stored and hold onto it for fear that it may drop out of the holster or pants. Both friend and foe are likely to engage in such tell-tale body language.

That point leads back to the second question in trying to detect armed adversaries: how to tell whether an armed person is a friend or foe. The short answer, with plenty of exceptions, is that good guys wear holsters and bad guys do not. Criminals do not want to be found with a holster after they have committed a crime and thrown the gun away. They prefer to carry guns tucked into the waist of their pants, either in front or in back.

Like most tasks in executive protection, detecting armed people and judging whether they are potential adversaries calls for the use of brains, not brawn. The key is to watch people's hand movements, eye movements, and other body language. A good exercise is to go to a crowded mall or busy street corner and watch people go by—and see if it is possible to pick out the individuals who may be carrying a gun, legally or otherwise.

Travel Considerations

Given the carry permit complications described earlier, armed protection when the principal is traveling can be problematic. Even if an EP specialist is licensed to carry a concealed firearm in both the home jurisdiction and the destination, transporting the weapon legally can be difficult (especially with air travel). The Law Enforcement Officers' Safety Act somewhat eases those complications for active and retired law enforcement officers working in the EP field, but the act does not apply outside the United States.

A good solution is to contract with an off-duty police officer who is trained in EP or with a licensed EP specialist in the destination city. That person, who can be the designated armed member of the protective detail, brings other advantages to the team, as well. He or she knows the local area, knows people to contact for emergency help, and is trained to use the weapon carried. It is even more desirable to contract with a police officer who is trained in EP practices, as are some law enforcement officers who have the duty to protect local or state dignitaries, such as a mayor or governor. This person's job would be to intervene if necessary so the regular EP staff can concentrate on moving the principal out of the danger zone.

Any outsider who is contracted to assist the protective detail must, as a condition of the job, show proof of his or her permission to carry a firearm, permission to work off-duty, permission to be the armed member of a private protective detail, and current range qualification. The person should also state what type of weapon and ammunition will be carried, and those tools must be the right type for the job. Once the EP team arrives on-site, the lead EP specialist should inspect the contractor and his or her paperwork to ensure that everything is in order.

Contracting with an armed, off-duty or retired law enforcement officer is a significant help for domestic travel. When the principal must be protected outside his or her home country, outside contractors are indispensable if armed protection is desired, as it is next to impossible to obtain a concealed carry permit abroad.

Step-Down Weapons

A protective detail need not choose between carrying firearms and being completely unarmed. A middle option is to carry step-down or less-lethal weapons. The following are a few of those weapons:

- TASER, a device that shoots two probes a short distance (about 15 feet) and then transmits pulsed energy that overwhelms the subject's central nervous system, causing immediate incapacitation
- ASP telescoping baton, which can be collapsed for easy concealment and expanded for use as an impact weapon
- Chemical sprays, including various pepper sprays
- Gladius, a "handheld tactical illumination tool" that operates like a flashlight but is also capable of delivering a high-output strobe effect to disorient adversaries
- Minuteman First Responder ballistic shield, which when

folded up looks like a briefcase but when expanded is a 2 foot by 4 foot bullet-resistant shield with an armored viewport; an unusual device, it can be a valuable defensive tool for covering the principal

Any step-down weapons carried on a protective detail must be approved in advance by the EP program. It is important that other members of the team know what weapons their colleagues are carrying and be familiar with the use and effects of such weapons. Moreover, the EP manager should gather information about laws in the local jurisdiction (and any jurisdictions to which the principal may travel) regarding step-down weapons in order to help EP staff comply with those laws. Certain step-down weapons are not allowed in some cities and facilities.

Step-down weapons cannot replace firearms where firearms are warranted. However, they offer certain benefits over firearms: they can be taken to many more places without legal difficulty; they are less likely to injure innocent bystanders; and they are particularly effective in close-quarters conflicts.

7.
Technology in Protective Operations

Remarkable technological tools have become readily available to EP specialists in recent years. Such tools help EP staff accomplish many tasks efficiently. The following are just a few of the EP chores that have been made much easier with new technology:

- communicating with other EP specialists and the principal
- locating the principal
- finding directions
- photographing security-significant scenes and sharing the photos with others
- providing advanced medical assistance

- setting up temporary security alarm systems
- obtain threat information on the go

Without a doubt, technology can be extraordinarily useful. The challenge is to use technological tools without becoming distracted by them or overly dependent on them. The EP specialist's most important tool is his or her mind, not cell phone. It takes time to learn how to use most technological devices well, they have a habit of breaking down at inconvenient moments, and they may be difficult to use well in a crisis. Still, the right use of technology can give an EP operation a definite edge over adversaries.

A single book chapter cannot cover all the new technologies that have become available to EP operations. Moreover, because of the speed of innovation and development, the list of technological tools grows daily, so any list of such tools is likely to become outdated fast. Therefore, this chapter focuses less on particular tools and more on the ways in which technology can be used in protective operations. Each section of the chapter describes a category of usage and names some of the tools in that category. Over time, an EP specialist may need to ask colleagues or search the World Wide Web to discover the latest tools in a given category, but the categories themselves—the ways in which technology can be used—should remain fairly constant. Those categories are as follows:

- communication
- navigation
- tracking
- photography
- information gathering
- alarm systems
- emergency response

Of course, those categories cannot be construed strictly, as some technologies are used in ways that could fit into several categories. Moreover, people—including both EP specialists and adversaries—think up new ways to use existing technologies every day.

Communication

Who can imagine life without mobile telephones? Like other technologies, they have quickly changed from novelty to necessity. They are probably the most valuable technology in executive protection. EP specialists can use them to

- stay in touch with home base when they are moving the principal from point to point,
- call ahead to colleagues at the destination to make sure the site is safe for the principal's arrival,
- call airlines, restaurants, hotels, and other resources to make plans, change plans, and work out any special assistance the principal may need,
- stage efficient pickups and handoffs with other members of the EP team, and
- coordinate many other activities.

Likewise, e-mail (at the office, at home, and while traveling) is an effective tool for sending EP colleagues directions, schedules, itineraries, and queries. E-mail is especially useful for travel to other time zones, as one can time-shift one's messages and not wake colleagues or the principal as one might with a mobile phone.

Voice and data communication are facilitated by international mobile telephones, satellite telephones (which work even when no cell towers are nearby), push-to-talk mobile telephones with group call features (making the phone more like a two-way radio for quick contact and for contact with several colleagues at once), wireless-capable notebook computers, and mobile e-mail devices like the Blackberry and e-mail capable mobile phones and personal digital assistants (PDAs).

A related technology is encryption, which protects voice and data communication. Few private-sector details employ encryption for their voice or data communications, but if the threat level warrants that degree of protection, it is available.

One technology, the OnStar system, could fit into many of this chapter's technology categories but will be presented here.[40] OnStar (available in most General Motors vehicles and some vehicles made by Audi, Acura, Isuzu, Lexus, Saab, Subaru, and Volkswagen) offers many services of great use to an EP detail. The system combines global positioning system (GPS) technology with a high-strength, vehicle-based mobile telephone to provide such services as the following:[41]

- automatic notification of air bag deployment (if front air bags deploy, the vehicle automatically sends a signal to OnStar and an advisor attempts to contact the vehicle's occupants; if they do not respond, the advisor contacts emergency services)
- vehicle diagnostics
- remote door unlocking
- notification of emergency services
- stolen vehicle location assistance
- roadside assistance
- accident assistance
- remote activation of horn and lights (to help locate the car)
- virtual advisor (a way of getting traffic and weather information)
- driving directions
- convenience services (restaurant recommendations, hotel locations, taxi calls, airline reservations, event tickets, etc.)

---

[40] There are some other, similar services, but at present OnStar is by far the best known.

[41] *OnStar Services*, retrieved April 23, 2006, from http://www.onstar.com/us_english/jsp/explore/onstar_basics/services.jsp.

Navigation

One of EP's most valuable contributions to a corporation is the service of moving the principal quickly and safely from one place to another. Both speed and safety are served when the EP driver knows several routes between points. With good, up-to-date navigation information, the EP driver can improve the likelihood of avoiding traffic jams and dangerous neighborhoods. Such information also makes it easier to choose alternate routes (to avoid predictability) and to navigate unfamiliar cities.

In EP today, with GPS technology and on-line mapping, there is little excuse for getting lost. GPS tools can guide a driver from point to point and recalculate directions in case of a wrong turn or traffic jam. Such devices, with voice directions and heads-up displays, make it relatively safe to follow directions. Instead of looking down at a map, the driver can watch the road.

GPS technology is embedded in factory-installed and aftermarket vehicle-based systems; in handheld devices; in notebook computers; and in mobile phones.

Navigation is also made easier through Web-based mapping services, such as those provided by Yahoo!, MapQuest, and Google. Such services, which provide not only maps but turn-by-turn directions, are available through computers linked to the Internet via hardwire (at the office) or wireless (on the road) connections. Mapping services are also accessible through Web-enabled mobile phones and PDAs.

Tracking

The same GPS technology used in the communication and navigation tools described earlier can also be used to track items and persons under the care of the EP program. For example, some mobile phones contain GPS technology that makes it possible for the EP operation to track the location of the person carrying the phone. Some companies provide GPS-equipped phones to their principals who travel to dangerous destinations. If a principal is kidnapped, it will be possible to determine his or her location to within a few feet as long as the phone is still with the principal.

A similar concept is employed in GPS watches and bracelets. Used mainly for children of protectees, those devices make it possible to track wearers who have been kidnapped or are missing for some other reason. Some GPS watches and bracelets are made so that they cannot easily be removed without a key.

Photography

Digital photography is an incredible boon to EP practitioners. They can easily take pictures or video of suspicious persons or vehicles, license plates, building exteriors and interiors (for security planning), contractors (such as limo drivers), and even documents. The images can then be e-mailed immediately to EP colleagues or others who need the information—even to law enforcement agencies.

Digital photography is an excellent tool in advance work (see Chapter 8: Know Before You Go), enabling the advance agent to send still pictures or video of locations, drivers, contract security personnel, and other resources to the principal or to EP staff who will accompany the principal on the trip. That way, the travelers will know what and whom to expect when they arrive. An EP program can also easily circulate be-on-the-lookout photos to EP staff, e-mailing the photos to their mobile telephones, PDAs, notebook computers, or other devices.

EP specialists can now take high-quality digital still photos and video with compact cameras, camera phones, and some PDAs. Digital photography is evolving fast, so better and smaller cameras are certainly on the way.

Information Gathering

Technology greatly enhances an EP specialist's ability to gather information that is vital to carry out the protective mission. From the World Wide Web (both free and fee sites) to Usenet newsgroups and e-mail, the Internet provides a deep source of practical data. EP specialists can easily find crime statistics, satellite and street-level photos, travel risk information, specific threat data, logistical support information, and much more. The information can be sought through and stored in computers, personal digital assistants (PDAs), and web-capable mobile phones. PDAs are especially useful as portable repositories for much of the information found, including such information as dates, directions, names and numbers of contacts, photographs, etc.

Technology aids information gathering in two main categories: risk assessment and travel support. When conducting a risk assessment (as described in Chapter 3), one can search the Web and various newsgroups to learn the answers to such questions as these:

- How well is the principal known?
- What are people's attitudes toward the principal?
- Who are the principal's family members?
- Are photos of the principal and his or her family members available?
- Are the principal's home address and phone number available?
- Are addresses and phone numbers available for any secondary homes the principal might own?
- Is the principal known to have significant wealth?
- How do people feel about the principal's employer?
- What is the level of crime around the principal's office and home?
- Have any fringe organizations taken an unfavorable position on the principal?

The second category in which technology greatly aids EP information gathering is travel support. Aside from the travel-related benefits in communication, navigation, tracking, and photography mentioned earlier, technology also helps with travel planning and coordinating.

From the Web, an EP specialist can obtain a variety of useful travel information:

- contact information for any hotels at which the principal might stay, plus names of nearby hotels that could serve as backup

- maps, satellite photos, and street-level photos of the hotel, meeting site, restaurants, and other locations that the principal will visit on the trip

- weather reports, including updated, moving radar maps, for almost anyplace in the world

- details of the often-changing Transportation Security Administration rules on items that may and may not be transported aboard aircraft

- travel risk information from numerous sources

In addition, with satellite radio (such as XM or Sirius), an EP specialist can obtain updated traffic, news, and weather reports for many major cities in the United States. That data makes it possible to conduct better planning for the principal's movements (to work, to the office, to meetings, etc.) and to develop and follow alternate strategies as traffic, weather, and local events change throughout the day.

Numerous travel risk information sources are available on the Web. Below is further information about two of the most significant sources: the Overseas Security Advisory Council (OSAC) of the U.S. Department of State and a fee-based service called iJET.

Overseas Security Advisory Council

OSAC (www.osac.gov) was formed to promote security cooperation between American business and private sector interests worldwide and the U.S. Department of State. OSAC has more than 3,500 member organizations and over 100 country councils. Much of its information is available on-line (hence the inclusion of OSAC's description in this chapter on technology), yet much of OSAC's benefit is not technology-based but arises from various briefing meetings and opportunities to network with people who face concerns similar to one's own.

OSAC's objectives are as follows:

- to establish continuing liaison between State Department security functions and the private sector

- to provide for regular and timely interchange of information between the private sector and the State Department concerning developments in the overseas security environment

- to recommend methods and provide material for coordinating security planning

- to recommend methods of protecting the competitiveness of American businesses operating worldwide

The increase in terrorism over the last 25 years and the continuing threat against U.S. interests overseas has led many American companies to seek help from the federal government, particularly the State Department. In 1985, several chief executive officers from prominent American companies met with then-Secretary of State George P. Shultz to promote cooperation between the American private sector worldwide and the U.S. government on security issues. The result was the establishment of OSAC.

OSAC is co-chaired by the director of the Diplomatic Security Service and a selected private sector representative. The organization's strategic plan calls for protecting American interests overseas by promoting public–private security partnerships through leadership, information sharing, and innovation.

OSAC uses technical advisors from the Federal Bureau of Investigation, National Security Agency, Office of the National

Counterintelligence Executive, Transportation Security Administration, U.S. Department of Homeland Security, U.S. Secret Service, U.S. Coast Guard, and U.S. Department of State.

In the fall of each year, OSAC hosts a major meeting for its constituents. Held at U.S. State Department headquarters in Washington, DC, the meeting features keynote speakers like the U.S. Secretary of State, as well as security briefings on various regions of the world. The invitation-only meeting also provides an opportunity for the private sector and public sector to network and share ideas and information.

With help from the U.S. Department of Commerce, OSAC established the Research and Information Support Center (RISC) in 1997. The RISC staff works with the private sector, the Bureau of Diplomatic Security and other federal agencies, and U.S. diplomatic missions around the world on matters of security involving U.S. firms and their employees. RISC gauges threats to U.S. private sector investment, personnel, facilities, and intellectual property abroad. With access to a broad range of classified and unclassified reporting from American embassies abroad, as well as open-source information, RISC can track social, political, and economic issues that affect the security of the private sector operating overseas.

The OSAC Web site is operated and maintained by the State Department's Bureau of Diplomatic Security. The site is the focal point for the exchange of unclassified information between the U.S. Department of State and the private sector on security-related incidents and threats overseas. The site provides the following, among other offerings:

- travel warnings and public announcements
- daily security-related news articles
- reports on security and crime incidents overseas
- terrorist group profiles
- timely information on terrorist attacks and other incidents

- general crime information for cities and countries
- contacts at U.S. posts overseas
- updates on new or unusual situations
- cyber threat information

OSAC members can enroll in the Foreign Service Institute's Private Sector Security Overseas Seminar, a two-day security awareness primer available to American citizens working for U.S. private sector organizations. The seminar takes place at the National Foreign Affairs Training Center in Arlington, Virginia. It covers travel, home and personal security, fire and environmental hazards, kidnap avoidance, cross-cultural competence, weapons of mass destruction, current threat trends, and crisis management.

It is not difficult to become an OSAC member. OSAC "constituency" is available to any American-owned, not-for-profit organization, or any enterprise incorporated in the U.S. (parent company, not subsidiaries or divisions) doing business overseas. The company must designate one representative from its U.S. headquarters to be the point of contact. Usually that designated representative is a corporate security director, but it could certainly be the EP manager.

After receiving an organization's application, OSAC verifies its eligibility. If the organization meets the criteria, it becomes a constituent and can send a representative to OSAC meetings and access the protected portions of the OSAC Web site. OSAC also grants access to its Web site to all federal, state, and local law enforcement agencies. An application can be submitted at http://www.osac.gov/Registration/index.cfm?display=userForm. The mailing address is Overseas Security Advisory Council, Bureau of Diplomatic Security, U.S. Department of State, Washington, DC 20522-2008. Telephone: (571) 345-2223.

iJET International, Inc.

iJET (www.ijet.com) is a private-sector, fee-based service that provides constantly updated travel risk information. The author sits on the security advisory board of iJET, which provides clients with several useful tools:

- **Worldcue® PRO.** Worldcue® PRO provides access to iJET's proprietary Travel Intelligence® database with continuously updated, destination-specific advisories and intelligence for 183 countries and 282 cities worldwide. It covers 10 categories of intelligence, including security, health, transportation, entry and exit, culture, weather and environment, financial, and communications. Worldcue® PRO also allows for real-time notifications and alerts. Clients can be notified of travel alerts immediately by region, country, or city and receive changes to selected country security assessment ratings.

- **Worldcue® Report Suite.** iJET reports provide analysis of changing risks facing clients' interests around the world. The service includes daily reporting of global situations, monthly reporting of regional trends, and timely special reports on emerging global concerns. Commentary and multi-source analysis by intelligence professionals helps clients assess their risks and respond appropriately.

- **Access to Analysts.** Clients can talk with iJET's regional analysts and subject matter experts for quick answers.

iJET runs a major, 24/7 intelligence operations center in Annapolis, Maryland. The center features automated collection systems that scan Web sites, process news feeds, and handle field reports from hundreds of human sources on the ground. Selected information is routed to the appropriate regional desk officer or subject matter expert. If the information is time-sensitive and actionable, an alert is produced; if not, the information is used to update the country and city databases.

Alarm Systems

Numerous portable wireless security systems have been developed in recent years. EP programs can use them to set up temporary security arrangements for aircraft, watercraft, vehicles, hotel doors, and other short-term applications.

Available systems offer a variety of wireless devices that sense motion, vibration, heat, smoke, breaking of light beams, "man down" (for someone working alone), and other conditions. In response, the sensors wirelessly transmit a signal to the user's receiving station. They may sound a chime, activate a voice message, play a recording of a barking dog, send a text message or e-mail, broadcast a message on the EP team's radio system, or call the user's mobile phone. Similar systems can wirelessly transmit closed-circuit television images so the EP team can see what is happening at the protected site.

These systems make it possible for EP staff to supplement the security systems already in place at various sites, to secure unsecured sites, and to establish a security perimeter around any type of object or site. Most can also be linked to a portable, personal alarm (a panic button) that the principal use to summon help as needed.

Emergency Response

Several medical technology developments particularly affect EP programs. It is important to remember that medical risks are at least as likely to harm most principals as are deliberate attacks. Therefore, emergency medical care is a key responsibility of EP specialists.

Automated External Defibrillators

One of the fastest-growing developments is the rise in the use of automated external defibrillators (AEDs). Those devices have become affordable (now costing $1,000 to $1,500) and are now seen in shopping malls, executive vehicles, aircraft, airports, offices, and other spaces where a user could easily find them to assist a person suffering from sudden cardiac arrest (SCA).

If necessary, an untrained Good Samaritan can use the kit to help a heart attack victim, but AED effectiveness is even greater if the user has been trained. As the American Red Cross puts it:[42]

> Training is necessary in order to understand the role of defibrillation in the broader context of the cardiac chain of survival. Training in CPR and AED skills will enable the rescuer to use all the steps in the cardiac chain of survival, thereby significantly increasing the victim's chance of survival. The cardiac chain of survival is a series of four critical steps. All four steps of the chain must be present to help ensure survival from sudden cardiac arrest. The four steps are:
>
> - Step one: Early access to care (calling 9-1-1 or another emergency number)
>
> - Step two: Early cardiopulmonary resuscitation (CPR)
>
> - Step three: Early defibrillation
>
> - Step four: Early advanced cardiac life support, as needed
>
> The third step, delivering an electrical shock to the heart, which is known as defibrillation, is recognized as the most critical step in restoring cardiac rhythm and resuscitating a victim of SCA.

DNA Identification Kits

DNA identification technology has quickly evolved from futuristic to commonplace. In executive protection, the technology is used as a means of identification in case the principal is kidnapped. In addition, it is common to prepare DNA kits for principals' family members. Having a DNA sample stored away could also be useful for identifying a body or, of course, solving certain crimes.

---

[42] American Red Cross, "Saving a Life Is as Easy as A-E-D," retrieved April 24, 2006, from http://www.redcross.org/services/hss/courses/aed.html#easy.

EP specialists do not have to become geneticists to use a DNA kit correctly. One kit, the Amber Alert DNA/ID kit, includes materials for taking a DNA sample (by swabbing inside the mouth), preserving the sample for up to 28 years, taking fingerprints, recording dental data and a physical description of the subject, and storing a photo of the subject.

The kits are inexpensive (approximately $10–$30) and can provide invaluable information for law enforcement agencies in the event of a kidnapping, homicide, or other such crime. The kits can be ordered at http://codeamber.org/dnakits.html.

Technology is a tool that, in the right hands, can improve an EP specialist's performance and save time. However, it does not take the place of real experience on the ground, and one must exercise good judgment in using it. For example, cell phones would seem indispensable, yet they can also become a distraction—if the EP specialist is talking on the phone instead of paying attention to the job at hand. When the author leads an EP detail that is actively working a principal, he tells his EP team to keep their mobile phones on the vibrate/no-ring setting. He explains that the only calls they should accept are calls from the leader or another member of the detail.

Another opportunity to use good judgment involves GPS navigation systems in vehicles. Such systems are truly useful, but their voice directions have some drawbacks. In the vehicle, the principal wants to work or relax, not listen to audible directions. Likewise, seeing the EP specialist squint constantly at the GPS display does not inspire the principal's confidence. The EP specialist should know the route and be paying attention to the road and all surroundings, not a little screen.

Driving route maps from the Internet, obviously helpful in many cases, may lead the party through crime-ridden neighborhoods or traffic snarls. Good judgment dictates that the EP specialist drive the routes in advance to determine the best ones.

In sum, technology is a tool to be used along with good judgment, not instead of it.

8.
Know Before You Go

This book's predecessor, *The Art of Executive Protection*, featured a chapter on the principles and methods of the advance. The significance of the advance was explained as follows:[43]

> What is an advance? Its definition is the totality of an EP specialist's efforts to learn about an executive's route and destination and all the details that affect the trip and the stay. Its practical effect is a *preemptive strike against confusion and exposure*. Advance work requires that a member of the protection team actually go to the destination and prepare the way. However, advance work does not apply solely to long-distance travel. Any location that the client intends to visit should be advanced—even if it's just across the street. An agent who has done a proper advance has a much better chance of keeping his protectee—and himself—out of trouble. Further, when a

---

[43] R. L. Oatman, *The Art of Executive Protection* (Baltimore, Maryland: Noble House, 1997), pp. 123-124.

threatening event occurs, he knows how to remove the client from the situation, whom to summon for help, and where to get medical or any other type of assistance, depending on the situation.

Experienced EP specialists strongly emphasize the importance of advance work. When two protective agents are available, it is almost always best to assign one to conduct an advance and one to accompany the principal, as opposed to assigning both to accompany the principal. Advance work is that important.

To help readers better understand the concept of advance work, this chapter describes a sample trip to Mexico City by a corporate executive from the United States. It uses that sample story to illustrate the following aspects of the advance:

- pre-advance
- airport advance
- ground transportation advance
- route advance
- lodging advance

In addition, this book provides actual sample advance checklists that EP specialists can use to capture their advance research. Checklists, while no substitute for on-the-ground judgment, are an invaluable tool for capturing details about a site, ensuring that no key steps are overlooked, and preserving information that can be used on future trips.

The advance checklists are presented in the appendix and, as a special free benefit to readers, are also available in electronic form for easy use and reproduction. To obtain the on-line checklists, readers should follow these simple instructions:

1. Go to www.rloatman.com/book_downloads
2. A security window will pop up. Please type in the following username and password exactly as shown:
   Username: surveys
   Password: ep$pecialist

3. A web page will open, listing the advance checklists included in this book
4. Click the link to the desired checklist
5. The reader's own copy of the survey is now ready for use

The checklists are periodically updated to reflect the latest thinking in executive protection. Readers are encouraged to download all the surveys and save them to their own computers for off-line use.

After studying the examples and principles that follow, EP staff should conduct a tabletop exercise to practice planning for a hypothetical trip by their principal. Such an exercise gives the team a chance to consider how they would gather the necessary information and who would execute the various steps. The exercise might well point up unknown strengths and weaknesses in the EP program that could be rectified before the next major trip is scheduled.

Sample Trip

The following story, based on actual events but changed in a few details to protect the principal's privacy, shows how an executive protection team approaches the planning for a principal's trip to a relatively high-risk destination. Its lessons apply equally to in-house EP operations and outside EP firms.

An independent EP firm receives a call from the chief of staff of a *Fortune* 50 company, a manufacturing business with plants in Mexico. He wants the firm to provide a security detail for his company's chief executive officer and two senior-level employees who will be traveling from Washington, DC, to Mexico City on business. The chief of staff explains that the company already has contract security officers at its Mexico facilities but, because of concerns about criminal activity (especially kidnapping and street crime) in that country, wants the temporary help of a company that specializes in executive protection. The party of three will stay at the J. W. Marriott Hotel in Mexico City—relatively near two of the company's plants—and also wants to make a side trip to visit a third plant in Guadalajara, some 300 miles away. Moreover, the three principals cannot count on any security support from the Guadalajara plant manager, as they want their visit to be a surprise.

When EP personnel are approached about such a project, they are also normally asked how much it will cost and how many personnel will be needed to make the trip a safe one. It is not wise to answer those questions immediately. Rather, the EP manager should wait until he or she has developed a better understanding of the detail's requirements. In fact, it is better not to accept the task (not so easy for in-house EP staff) if the job seems beyond the EP team's abilities. In some cases, the best course of action is to tell the in-house or external client that the trip requires resources (such as staffing and local knowledge) that the EP operation does not possess. Of course, that statement should be followed by an offer to help the client find the necessary resources, such as an EP firm with experience in the destination area. The client will appreciate the honest answer and will return to ask for assistance in the future. However, if the EP manager feels confident that the EP team possesses or can subcontract for the necessary expertise, it is time to begin planning.

An ideal condition for a successful mission is to have the on-site advance work performed by a trained executive protection specialist who lives and works in the location that is to be visited. It is possible to provide a protective detail without such a resource, but the likelihood of success is far greater when a local EP specialist is made part of the team.

In the sample story, the EP manager explains to the chief of staff that an EP specialist from the EP firm will accompany the principals on the trip and be supported, before and during the trip, by an EP specialist who lives and works in Mexico City.

Under that arrangement, one senior security person will act as the client's point of contact, get to know the principals' needs, and develop the security plan with input from the chief of staff. The chief of staff and principals will only have to get to know one EP specialist, an English speaker who by now knows their needs. In turn, that EP specialist will be supported, somewhat behind the scenes, by the Mexico City–based EP specialist. Together, the two EP agents can provide seamless, non-intrusive protection that does not draw attention to the principals and, by smoothing logistics, helps them make the best use of their time.

A challenge for the security provider is to educate and not lecture the potential client about personal protection. A face-to-face meeting is preferred but not always possible. The EP manager should be prepared to give a general description of the protection approach that will be taken and the information and support he will need from the client. In executive protection, knowledge truly is power.

Pre-Advance

The next step is the pre-advance. The term may sound redundant, but in EP it means the preparatory work that one does before sending someone to the site (the advance) before the principal's visit. In the pre-advance, one asks specific questions like these:

- What is going on today, tomorrow, and next week in the city to which the executive is traveling?
- Who can help the EP team there?
- What airports, roads, hotels, and vehicles will the EP team use?
- What threats lurk at the destination?

At this point, the EP manager asks the chief of staff or his or her designee to gather as much information as possible about the principals to build a proper protective platform. The EP team can best plan security if it knows the following:

- basic biographical information about the principals (such as name, position and title in the company, controversial aspects, special medical conditions or needs, home address, date of birth, emergency contacts, recent photograph, fingerprints, voice recording, DNA sample, religion, and copy of passport)
- their itineraries and daily schedules during the trip (so the security detail can plan for each movement)
- the purpose of the trip
- lodging requirements
- desired mode of transportation
- any known or suspected potential threats to the company or the principals
- the need for any side trips the principals might wish to take
- company's medical evacuation plan, if any, and applicability of medical insurance outside the principal's home country
- intention to use private versus commercial aircraft

The EP manager then supplies a form that the principals can use to record additional, more detailed information about themselves. This record is to be kept in the client company's possession, maintained in privacy and accessed only in case of emergency. The table on the following page shows the type of information that should be collected.

Personal Data to Collect for Use in Case of Emergency	
Name	Driver's license (state, county, number, expiration date)
Title	Passport (country, number, expiration date)
Office location	
Photos of principal, spouse, and children	Similar information about spouse
Physical description, including scars or identifying marks	Household staff (position, name, address, phone number, nationality, driver's license number, passport number)
Date and place of birth	
Address and phone number for primary and secondary residences	Personally owned vehicles (make/type, year, color, state, registered owner, license number, insurance carrier, policy number)
Mobile phone numbers	
Special medication requirements and drug allergies	Locations, contact names, phone numbers, and schedules for regular events (e.g., children's schools, teachers, and principals)
Doctor, dentist, and pharmacy names, addresses, and phone numbers	

In addition, the principal might appreciate the EP specialist's recommendation to complete a medical power of attorney form. By using the form, the principal designates someone to make medical decisions for him or her if the principal is incapable of making those decisions.

After gathering the initial information from the client company, the EP manager reviews notes from any prior trips he may have taken with the same or different principals to that destination (if possible). This is the time to pull out the EP program's old advance file and look for pertinent data. Details from an old advance file cannot simply be cut and pasted into a new advance file, but the old information can at least provide a starting point in the research.

Once the EP manager has in hand the old advance (if one exists) and the necessary information from the principals, it is time to begin fresh, trip-specific research. As was discussed in Chapter 7: Technology in Protective Operations, the Internet is a profound benefit to EP specialists who are looking to collect key information about the destination, such as the following:

- routes
- hotels
- restaurants
- airports
- impending strikes that might cripple transportation or other essential services
- crime rates
- new types of crimes (e.g., express kidnapping, being pulled over by criminals in police uniforms, etc.)
- hospitals and any current epidemics
- recommended or required vaccinations
- police stations and fire departments
- political climate
- actual (weather) climate
- passport and visa requirements
- U.S. embassy or consulate
- holidays
- cultural information

For the planned Mexico City trip, the EP manager gathers the preceding information and then calls or e-mails the regional security officer (RSO) at the U.S. embassy in Mexico City (or at a U.S. consulate in other Mexican cities), explains that he will be providing protection and logistical support for a VIP, and asks for any suggestions or other information that he should know.

As Chapter 7 mentioned, up-to-date information about travel risks associated with any destination can be obtained from several sources. For example, the Overseas Security Advisory Council

(OSAC) of the U.S. Department of State has a Web site (www.ds-osac.org) that provides critical information regarding crime and terrorist activity as well as tips for traveling safely to various destinations.

Information for the pre-advance (and during the duration of the trip) can also be obtained from for-profit security intelligence providers. For example, iJET International, Inc. (www.ijet.com), can provide a wealth of information to any EP specialist planning a principal's trip.

Airport Advance

Most airports have Web sites that show the general layout of the airport, including the location of the various terminals; hours of operation; available services, such as restaurants, lodging, and shopping; the location of any airline clubs; parking and pickup/drop-off locations; contact information for requests for VIP handling for the principal; customs and immigration requirements; and contact information for airport security and law enforcement.

For security planning purposes, the EP manager clearly needs to know which airport the principals intend to use. In this case, if the principals are flying on a commercial aircraft, they will likely land at the Mexico City Benito Juarez International Airport. If they use private aircraft, they will probably fly into Adolfo Lopez Mateos International Airport, also known as the Toluca airport, which is approximately one hour from central Mexico City.

The airport advance, conducted either from afar by the main EP team or from the actual site by the team's local EP contractor, will show, for example, that Adolfo Lopez Mateos International Airport is controlled by the army because of drug trafficking concerns. A Federal Judicial Police officer boards each corporate flight before departure to conduct a head count and compare it to the flight manifest. Security officers employed by the airport protect any unattended corporate aircraft.

The advance should provide information that will enable the EP team to speed the principals through immigration and customs checkpoints. The local EP contractor can be especially helpful in working out those details in advance, as well as arranging luggage to be collected in a way that does not leave the principals standing around crowded luggage carousels in a crowded, hectic environment.

Proper advance work is essential to a smooth trip. EP specialists have good reason not to like surprises, and diligent advance work goes a long way toward minimizing unforeseen events.

More guidance regarding air travel security considerations is provided in Chapter 10: Long-Distance Travel.

Ground Transportation Advance

The ground transportation advance provides useful details on moving the principals around once they complete their flight. Before the principals ever leave home, the EP manager works out who will drive (e.g., a driver from normal car service or a trained security driver), whether a standard or protected vehicle will be used, how the arriving principals will be located and picked up in a way that does not draw attention or make them vulnerable to kidnappers, and how their luggage will be transported (e.g., moved with the principals or taken separately to the hotel).

On the sample Mexico City trip, the principals are escorted through the airport by the primary EP specialist. He may have traveled with them, or he may have flown down beforehand to meet them. The principals recognize him because they have already met him or have at least seen a photograph of him. Once the principals exit the secured zone of the airport, the primary or local EP specialist escorts them directly into waiting vehicles. No signs identify the executives, and because arrangements have been made for the luggage, they do not need to stand around waiting for the bags. The principals are quickly escorted to a car with a trained security driver. The vehicle's engine is running and the doors are locked.

Sorting out the ground transportation details in advance provides a great payoff in terms of security and convenience. Moving quickly and surely through the airport, not lingering for luggage, and climbing straight into a waiting vehicle reduces the principals' exposure to both street crime and crime that specifically targets the principals.

More guidance regarding ground transportation security considerations is provided in Chapter 9: Local Travel.

Route Advance

Before the principals are driven through the city, it is important that suitable routes be worked out. The EP specialist should be familiar with several routes for traveling from the airport to the hotel and the various stops on the principals' itinerary. Both primary and secondary routes should be driven in advance so the EP specialist can look for hazards (such as dangerous neighborhoods), choke points (where the principals would be especially vulnerable to attack), and other concerns. The route advance also provides an opportunity for the EP specialist to look for safe havens along the way (such as police stations, hospitals, or firehouses). If the EP specialist senses that the principals' car is being followed, it is good to know of places where the party can safely stop.

The vehicle should of course contain maps and, if possible, GPS technology, but those should be used only for backup or periodic confirmation of directions. Because the routes have been advanced, the driver should already know the best ways to travel while transporting the principals.

The route advance should also take into consideration the traffic patterns at the specific times of day at which the principals will need to be transported. The service of executive protection involves moving the principals from point to point not only safely but also on time.

Moreover, the primary EP specialist, local contract EP specialist, and security driver should plan together how they will respond to any problems along the route, whether small (traffic jam or aggressive panhandler) or large (attack by adversaries on a motorcycle). The security team's response will be much better if all the players know the plan.

In the Mexico City scenario, the principals expressed a desire to make a side trip to Guadalajara. Thus, the EP specialist needs to conduct a route advance for that city, as well.

Lodging Advance

The Internet has made lodging advances easier than ever. To protect the principals properly, the EP specialist needs to know the best route for bringing the principals into the hotel—in other words, the quickest route that will lead them past the fewest people. The EP specialist also needs to know his or her way around the hotel in order to be able to assist the principals and guide them quickly where they want to go. Guest rooms, meeting rooms, restaurants, and other hotel facilities need to be examined and their layout understood before the principals arrive.

Many hotel Web sites provide much of the information that the EP specialist needs. They also often shows pictures of the hotel's exterior, guest rooms, lobbies, meeting rooms, and other facilities. Advance familiarity with the hotel enables the EP specialist to check out the site's security vulnerabilities, positive security measures, and surroundings. Some of the needed information can be gained in advance over the Internet or through telephone conversations with the hotel's general manager and security director. For examine, it is relatively easy (but still essential) to find out the hotel's telephone and fax numbers, e-mail address, and available services. Other kinds of information can only be gained by a site visit. In some cases the advance hotel visit can be made by the local contract EP specialist. In other cases, the primary EP specialist travels to the destination a day or two ahead of the principals and takes the time to examine the hotel in person. During a site visit, the EP specialist can acquaint himself or herself with entry and exit options, fire escape routes, and both attractions and threats in the surrounding area.

Remember, advance checklists are presented both in the appendix and on-line at www.rloatman.com/book_downloads, where readers may freely download them for easy use. Readers who wish to obtain the checklists from the site must type in the following:

Username: surveys
Password: ep$pecialist

9.
Local Travel

Protecting principals would be much easier if they stayed in one place, shuttered behind many layers of security. Of course, they do not. They move around town, to their offices, to business meetings, to social functions, to restaurants, to airports, and then back home. Because all that moving around takes them out of their well-protected offices and homes, they are most exposed to adversaries when they are in transit. Moreover, given the rate of automobile crashes in most countries, driving or riding in a car is one of the more dangerous activities most people engage in.[44] Thus, one of the most important tasks in executive protection is to ensure safe local travel.

According to the National Highway Traffic Safety Administra-

---

[44] Fatality rates per passenger mile traveled vary greatly from country to country. Some countries have rates that are as much as 35 times higher than those of other countries. The EP specialist should look into those rates when assessing the risk of a trip to a given country.

tion,[45] for 2005 the number of persons *killed* in motor vehicle traffic crashes was projected to increase by about 1 percent compared to 2004, after two years of decline. The number of persons *injured* in motor vehicle traffic crashes was projected to decline by 4 percent. A different way to measure the dangers is to look at the fatality rate per vehicle miles traveled. Taking that view, the *fatality* rate per 100 million vehicle miles traveled (VMT) was projected to increase slightly, while the *injury* rate per 100 million VMT was projected to decrease slightly. The following tables contain more data on this subject:

U.S. Traffic Crash Data, 2004–2005			
	Year		% Change
	2004	2005 Projected	
Persons killed	42,636	43,200	+1.3%
Persons injured	2,788,000	2,675,000	-4.1%
Fatal crashes	38,253	38,963	+1.9%
Nonfatal crashes	6,143,000	5,897,000	-4.0%
Injury crashes	1,862,000	1,802,000	-3.2%
Property damage only	4,281,000	4,095,000	-4.3%
Note: Totals may not add due to rounding. Percentages computed after rounding. Sources: Fatality Analysis Reporting System and National Automotive Sampling System General Estimates System.			

[45] National Highway Traffic Safety Administration, "Motor Vehicle Traffic Crash Fatalities and Injuries, Based on the Fatality Analysis Reporting System (FARS) and the National Automotive Sampling System (NASS) General Estimates System (GES): 2005 Projections," retrieved April 4, 2006, from www.nhtsa.dot.gov.

146

U.S. Traffic Crash Fatalities and Injuries per 100,000 Vehicle Miles Traveled (VMT), 2004–2005			
	Year		% Change
	2004	2005 Projected	
Persons killed per 100M VMT	1.44	1.46*	+1.4%
Persons injured per 100M VMT	94	90*	-4.3%

Sources: Fatality Analysis Reporting System, National Automotive Sampling System General Estimates System, Federal Highway Administration, and Census Bureau.

The crime of carjacking, another risk to principals driving in high-end vehicles, is less in the news than it once was, but it is still a hazard to protect against. Statistics on carjacking are rare, as police departments do not necessarily record the crime under the name "carjacking." Still, according to a 2004 report from the Bureau of Justice Statistics,[46] based on the National Crime Victimization Survey, from 1993 to 2002, on average, about 38,000 carjacking victimizations occurred annually, a rate of 1.7 victimizations per 10,000 persons each year.

The following are some tips that EP specialists should pass along to their principals, who can practice them when they are not receiving protection:

- Be aware of your surroundings as you approach your car. If suspicious persons are near it, walk past it and go to a safe area.

---

[46] Patsy Klaus, "National Crime Victimization Survey: Carjacking, 1993-2002," Bureau of Justice Statistics, U.S. Department of Justice, NCJ 205123, July 2004. Retrieved May 4, 2006, from http://www.ojp.usdoj.gov/bjs/pub/ascii/c02.txt.

- For quicker entry into the car, have your keys ready as you approach it.

- If you had locked the car when you left it, but now it is unlocked or open, do not get in. Instead, summon help.

- Lock all the doors and keep windows closed once you have entered the car.

- If a stranger approaches you after you have entered the car, do not open a door or window. Drive away. Sound the horn if you feel threatened.

- Try not to drive through dangerous areas. To avoid becoming vulnerable due to a breakdown, keep the car in good repair and full of gas.

- Allow maneuvering room between your car and the vehicle in front of it.

- If someone attempts to stop your car or causes an accident in a potentially dangerous area, drive to a safe place, such as an occupied gas station or police station.

- If an unmarked police car attempts to stop you and you are not sure it is driven by a police officer, signal to the officer your intentions to drive to an area you believe is safe, such as an open convenience store or police station.

Few principals who are receiving executive protection would travel very far on foot or at all on public transportation. Nearly all local travel is by automobile, a mode that gives the protective program at least some control over the environment. One cannot directly control the behavior of other drivers or of adversaries, but one can largely control three other, very important factors in secure local transport: the driver, the route, and the vehicle.

The Driver

In a protective program, who drives the vehicle when the principal needs to travel across town? It could be the principal himself or herself, a chauffeur, a trained security driver, or an EP specialist. From a security standpoint, there are advantages and disadvantages to using each of those types of drivers. Moreover, the protective program must adjust the way it operates, depending on who is doing the driving.

Principal

Many principals like to drive their own vehicles to work and after business hours. From a protection standpoint, that approach may or may not be safe, depending on the findings of the risk assessment. However, principals may well resist being advised not to drive themselves. EP specialists must find a way to strike the right balance between offering their principals protective driving service and making any suggestions that sound like a withdrawal of driving privileges. Such suggestions, if poorly received, could ruin a principal's view of the whole protective program.

In most cases, principals feel comfortable driving to and from work. They are familiar with the route, they are glad to have a little time to themselves, and they may own cars that are particularly enjoyable to drive. However, EP staff should gently point out that an attack against a principal in an automobile is most likely to take place as the vehicle is arriving at or leaving the home or office. Those are predictable moments for adversaries. If the principal is doing the driving, he or she cannot duck down behind the back seat for cover during an attack.

There is also the issue of attentiveness. Almost anyone who drives the same or a similar route to and from work each day slips into autopilot mode now and then or even much of the time. When a driver is in that mode, he or she does not look for potential threats along the way. By contrast, a switched-on EP specialist or security driver constantly thinks "what if?" and makes response plans accordingly. The distracted principal, driving himself or herself, is unlikely to be skilled at paying attention to dangers on the road.

If the risk assessment concludes that at least some of the time the principal should be driven by another person, the EP specialist can point out the advantages of having a driver: quicker pickups and drop-offs (no need to sit through slow parking processes), as well as time to rest, think, read, or make mobile phone calls. In practice, most principals drive themselves after hours, and many principals who receive executive protection still drive themselves to and from work. The right answer depends on the work, home, and commuting environments; working hours; driving skill level of the principal; and other factors.

Regardless of whether principals drive themselves always, often, or only sometimes, it is wise to recommend that they (and in some cases their spouses) take at least a half-day course in defensive and evasive driving. Even if there is never a deliberate attack on a principal, he or she will be safer through learning and practicing a few specialized driving techniques. Most adults—even veteran drivers, including law enforcement and security professionals—are surprised to learn that there is more to driving than they had realized. With a little training, principals can learn to swerve more safely to avoid hazards, stop faster, and accelerate faster than they ever knew. A little training may go a long way toward protecting principals when they want to drive themselves. Chapter 11: Training and Certification presents information on security driving schools.

Chauffeur

Depending on the findings of the risk assessment, use of an ordinary driver or chauffeur may or may not provide sufficient protection for a principal. Basically, in an attack, an ordinary driver can focus on driving while the principal focuses on shielding himself. However, an ordinary driver cannot provide much more protection than that.

On out-of-town trips, if the principal will be transported around town by a professional driver, at least there is a good chance the driver will know the city well enough to navigate successfully. Still, using an ordinary driver mainly provides convenience, not security.

In practice, most ground transportation is arranged not by EP staff but by a principal's executive assistant. Alternatively, if the principal travels on private aircraft, ground transportation arrangements may be made by the flight crew. In both cases, the planners typically have no idea who will be picking up the principal.

Another concern is the use of car services when the principal travels alone to another city. The EP program may have seen to the principal's protection at home and at work, and may even have driven the principal to the airport, yet when the principal's plane lands, he or she will be picked up by an unknown person holding a sign with the principal's name on it. That is a glaring gap in security. For all the principal knows, the real driver could be in the trunk of the car, while the driver with the name card could be a kidnapper. (That is a kidnapping strategy often used in Latin America.) Even if there is no criminal concern, the EP staff responsible for the principal's safety is putting him or her into the hands of an unknown person. That is not a good solution. It is better to supply the principal or the EP specialist with a picture of the driver and to provide the driver with a picture of the principal or EP specialist. Next, the two parties should meet at a predetermined location away from where the majority of the public is standing and waiting for other arriving passengers.

Especially in the home city but even, possibly, in other cities to which the principal travels often, if the EP program has a long-term relationship with a particular driver who seems competent and dependable, it may make sense to send him or her to training in security driving and emergency medical response. The protective effort can be strengthened significantly if the driver has at least a few emergency or security skills beyond basic driving.

Trained Security Driver

The next step up in security is to use a trained security driver. Such a person is not a fully trained executive protection specialist. Rather, he or she is primarily a driver but has received training in security considerations (such as hazards to look for and the importance of varying the route), defensive and evasive driving, and first aid.

Training members of a corporate driving pool in security driving is a cost-effective way to increase protection for the principals. The driving then becomes more than just a convenience—it becomes a protective measure. Security driving courses are discussed further in Chapter 11: Training and Certification.

When a principal travels to another city and is not accompanied by an EP specialist, it is much better to place the principal in the care of a trained security driver than to leave him or her to the mercies of taxis or car services.

EP Specialist

A higher level of protection is obtained when the principal's trained security driver is also a fully trained EP specialist. An EP specialist/driver can drive the vehicle safely, look for possible hazards and attack opportunities, employ defensive and evasive driving, and also execute all the security responses expected of an EP specialist (e.g., physically covering the principal, removing the principal from harm, possibly even returning fire in the most extreme situations). The EP specialist should also have current training in first aid, including cardiopulmonary resuscitation and use of an automated external defibrillator. The expense of using an EP specialist as the principal's driver is not warranted in all cases, but when such a service is needed, it provides a greater degree of protection than allowing the principal to drive himself or herself or hiring a chauffeur or trained security driver.

The Route

The speed and solidity of an automobile provide some protection to a principal as he or she travels locally. However, the predictability of the vehicle's route can undermine much of that protection. It is easy for an adversary to figure out that the principal's vehicle will, for example, leave the home about 7:30 a.m. every weekday morning and leave the office garage about 6:00 p.m. every weekday evening. However, it is also easy for EP staff to know that arrival and departure at the home and office are vulnerable points—and to add human or electronic surveillance at those points.

By contrast, once the drive is under way, it is very difficult for the EP team to keep the environment under any certain degree of surveillance. One cannot post guards or mount closed-circuit television cameras along the entire route. On the other hand, it may not be easy for the adversary to determine where the vehicle will be at any given time. If the vehicle always takes the same route and stops at traffic signals or in predictable, recurring traffic jams, an adversary can probably identify some opportunities for an attack (for example, from a motorcycle or with a stationary explosive device planted along the route). If the vehicle takes varying routes, it is much more difficult for an adversary to identify opportunities for attack.

The recommendation to vary one's route is common in the security field. Sometimes it is easy to do, but in other cases there are few good alternative ways to reach one's destination. Still, varying the driving route is something to do as best one can.

In choosing and using all routes (not just between home and office), EP specialists should do the following:

- Identify as many as routes as possible. (Are there three, five, seven ways to get from home to work?)
- Minimize chokepoints. (Are there places where the vehicle is always going to be stopped or moving slowly and

would be vulnerable to attack, such as long traffic signals, stop signs, railroad crossings, drawbridges, school zones?)

- Maximize safe havens. (How far apart are the various points where the vehicle can stop to obtain help?)
- Maintain route logs to avoid patterns. (How often does the vehicle travel a given route? Does the vehicle predictably travel by one route on Mondays and another on Tuesdays?)
- Become familiar with features along the routes in order to be able to identify items or people that are out of the ordinary. (Why is that van parked near the traffic signal where the principal often stops?)
- Study traffic patterns. (What are the different traffic levels on weekdays, weekends, and holidays?)
- Stay abreast of special events planned in the area. (Will the drive be interrupted by a parade, demonstration, or sporting event?)
- Beware of overpasses. (Could someone drop a heavy object onto the vehicle from above?)

A GPS device may be helpful in planning alternate routes. The preceding considerations are important in the United States but even more so in extra high risk countries, where attacks from motorcycles or via stationary explosives are more common.

The Vehicle

More and more EP details are making use of protected or armored vehicles. In the past, such vehicles were unusual and available solely through special armoring companies, but today they are common enough to be sold by several major auto manufacturers in addition to armorers. When the risk level warrants a higher degree of protection, these vehicles significantly help EP specialists safeguard their principals.

Purpose

Basically, a protected automobile buys the driver and passengers some time. In an attack, it can provide a chance to escape, or it can serve as a safe haven briefly until help arrives. Because it is not easily disabled, the protected vehicle can keep driving even after an attack has started. Its radiator will not be knocked out, its tires can run flat, etc. If the car is pinned in by the attackers, it can provide a safe haven for a short time because its windows cannot easily be shot out and its door and roof panels are bullet-resistant. A protected vehicle can give its driver and passengers a sense of security—a realistic, valid sense of security.

Protected vehicles cost much more than unprotected vehicles of the same style. Why would an EP operation want to devote substantial resources to a protected vehicle? The following are several conditions that might call for its use:

- The principal lives in or often drives through a dangerous area.
- The principal is visiting a dangerous area.
- The principal or his or her company has recently become dangerously controversial.
- The principal or his or company has recently received threats.
- Special hazards have arisen, such as riots[47] or strikes.
- The protectee warrants a high level of protection but is in a location where his or her EP specialists are not allowed to carry firearms.

When a corporation's chief executive officer is at a stoplight and a criminal sticks his gun against the driver's side window, how

---

[47] Riots and large, unruly crowd scenes are not as rare as casual observers might think. In the United States, people may think back to the widespread riots of 1968. However, they may not immediately recall the 1992 Los Angeles riots, the 1999 Seattle riots, the 2001 Cincinnati riots, and the 2003 Benton Harbor, Michigan, riots.

much would the corporation pay for that window to be bullet-resistant? When thugs place glass and nails in the road to cause flat tires in a dangerous neighborhood, how much would the corporation pay for the principal to be able to keep driving to a place of safety? If the CEO lives in a safe part of town but routinely travels to a high-crime urban downtown to visit restaurants or attend the symphony, would the corporation not be happy to pay extra to keep him safe and functioning?

Again, a protected vehicle gives the principal an edge—an extra 5 to 10 seconds to get out of the kill zone based on the level of protection in the vehicle. In an attack, it is best to keep the car moving. If the principal drives a protected vehicle, it is important that he or she know its limitations. The principal who will drive a protected car should take training in how to operate that particular car in worst-case situations.

The conditions that justify the use of a protected vehicle could be ongoing or temporary. If they are ongoing, the EP operation may choose to purchase a protected vehicle. If the conditions seem to be temporary, the EP operation may choose to lease such a car. Prudent EP programs make rental or leasing arrangements well before a crisis develops.

Before helping the company purchase a protected vehicle, the EP specialist should do some homework, getting the views of other security professionals, touring the manufacturing or armoring facility, examining ballistic testing and the overall integrity of the product, and studying the vehicle's warranty.

Description

Contemporary protected automobiles do not draw attention to themselves. This is not a case of a security measure attracting the attention of criminals. These cars are not the humblest of vehicles, and sometimes they are 8–18 inches longer than their non-protected counterparts, but for the most part they look like other cars the principals are likely to drive.

Car armorers report that protected vehicles have changed significantly over the past two decades. Thomas Herlihy, national sales manager of Scaletta Moloney Armoring,[48] says his firm has learned to build better cars in reaction to rising threat levels. Vehicle design is responding to users' needs for protection against terrorist attacks, chemical attacks, and other threats. Mr. Herlihy observes that Scaletta Moloney Armoring is not merely attaching reinforcements onto cars; rather, it has become more of an engineering company in order to integrate new, useful security features into principal's vehicles.[49]

2004 Cadillac DeVille, armored by Scaletta Moloney Armoring, owned by author. Armored to NIJ Type IV standard (high-powered rifle).

Same vehicle, rear view.

Protected cars may be born or made. In other words, some vehicles are given armoring and other protective features by the factory that manufactures the cars. Example of auto manufacturers that sell factory-armored vehicles include General Motors (Cadillac DeVille), Ford (Lincoln Town Car), BMW, and Mercedes Benz. By contrast, other protected vehicles begin as standard cars and have special features added later by a specialized armoring company.

---

[48] www. scaletta.com.
[49] Interview with Thomas Herlihy, July 22, 2005.

Descriptions of protected cars often state that the vehicles' armoring materials meet standards set by the National Institute of Justice (the research arm of the U.S. Department of Justice). NIJ Standard 0108.01, Ballistic Resistant Protective Materials, classifies ballistic-resistant protective materials into five types by level of performance, based on the material's ability to resist penetration by various types of weapons and ammunition. Each level or type also protects against the threats defeated by the lower-ranked types. For example, Type III-A armor protects against .44 Magnum and 9 mm submachine gun rounds, as well as the rounds de-

View of 8-inch stretch.

feated by materials of Type I, Type II-A, and Type II. (The "A" designation means the armor is somewhat less resistant than a type designation without the A.) The classifications are as follows:[50]

- **Type I (.22 long rifle and .38 special).** This armor also provides protection against lesser threats, such as 12 gauge number 4 lead shot and most handgun rounds in calibers .25 and .32.

- **Type II-A (lower-velocity .357 magnum, as well as 9 mm).** This armor also provides protection against lesser threats, such as 12 gauge 00 buckshot, .45 automatic, .38 special, and some other factory loads in calibers .357 magnum and 9 mm.

---

[50] National Institute of Justice Technology Assessment Program, "Ballistic Resistant Protective Materials: NIJ Standard 0108.01," Washington, DC, 1985.

- **Type II (higher-velocity .357 magnum, as well as 9 mm).** This armor also protects against most other factory loads in caliber .357 magnum and 9 mm.

- **Type III-A (.44 magnum and 9 mm submachine gun).** This armor also provides protection against most handgun threats.

- **Type III (high-powered rifle).** This armor also protects against most lesser threats, such as .223 Remington (full metal jacket), .30 carbine (full metal jacket), and 12 gauge rifle slug.

- **Type IV (armor-piercing rifle).** This armor also provides at least single hit protection against all the threats mentioned above.

Thus, an NIJ Type II protected vehicle would safeguard its occupants from an attack using higher-velocity .357 magnum or 9 mm ammunition, as well as lesser ammunitions.

Bullet-resistant metal panels, windshields, and windows are not the only characteristics of a protected vehicle. Resisting a several-shot firearms attack is not enough. If the adversaries keep shooting, they will eventually defeat the armor. The protective goal is to withstand a few shots and still be able to flee the danger zone.

The following are some of the special features of various protected vehicles:

- more powerful engine to handle increased car weight ably
- stronger brakes to stop the heavier vehicle quickly
- special suspension to maintain good handling despite greater weight of vehicle
- self-sealing fuel tank to prevention explosion or loss of fuel due to punctures (and to preserve mobility)
- run-flat tires to preserve mobility for escape
- tailpipe cover
- dual battery system

- engine fire suppression system
- siren
- public address system
- inside/outside intercom
- reinforced bumpers for ramming
- supplemental oxygen
- remote start

EP programs clearly have many options when looking for ways to reduce their principals' ground transportation risks.

Driving Skills Needed

Protective driving requires specialized skills, typically developed through training at various driving schools. Such schools are discussed in Chapter 11: Certification and Training. EP specialists or others who plan to drive protected vehicles should also obtain specialized training in handling such cars.

Because armored vehicles may weigh more—sometimes thousands of pounds more—than comparable non-armored vehicles, they accelerate, brake, and handle differently. In a field like executive protection, where the best plan is to make no mistakes, EP specialists and security drivers who plan to drive a protected vehicle should make sure to take specialized training in handling such a heavy car. The newest protected vehicles handle much like non-protected vehicles, but gaining familiarity with the car's different dynamics—how it behaves in normal driving and also in an emergency—would better prepare the driver to protect the principal.

10.
Long-Distance Travel

EP specialists like to eliminate uncertainty. They make lists; they check and double-check their facts; they participate in training so they will be ready in crises. However, when a principal takes an out-of-town trip, the uncertainty level rises sharply. Reducing it to maximize security requires a vigorous, thoughtful effort by the EP program. This chapter examines general EP travel considerations, commercial travel, and private flight operations.

General EP Travel Considerations

Highlights of trip planning—including the process known as the advance—were described in Chapter 8: Know Before You Go. The present chapter examines travel preparations and considerations in greater detail.

Preparation

When the EP program learns about upcoming travel in the principal's plans, the first step is to determine the security parameters of the trip. Because the EP specialist is almost certain to be less familiar with conditions and contacts outside the country, foreign travel presents the greatest challenges. This is the time to seek answers to the following questions:

- What is the purpose of the trip: to visit a customer, meet a potential business partner, check out a potential takeover target, mediate a labor dispute, investigate employee wrongdoing, or fire a manager? The trip's purpose may make a significant difference. For example, if the principal is traveling to fire a plant manager, it would not be wise to place that person, who may suspect the purpose of the trip, in charge of security measures for the principal's visit.

- What is the general level of risk at the destination? For example, what is the level of terrorism and other crimes? Is there ongoing political and socioeconomic turmoil, some of which could even be targeted at the principal or what he or she represents? Are there significant disease and health concerns to develop protective strategies for?

- What temporary risk factors may affect the trip, such as demonstrations or riots at the destination, a heightened threat against aircraft due to terrorism, or a rash of kidnappings or carjackings?

- What characteristics of the principal might place him or her at greater than average risk there? Is there anything about the principal's identity, employer, net worth, nationality, or other factors that might make the principal an especially attractive or vulnerable target?

- What can be done to lower the principal's profile on the trip—to slip in and out of the destination without attracting much attention?

- In cases where keeping a low profile is impossible, what can be done to harden the principal as a target?

Coordination and Rapport

Executive protection for a principal's domestic or overseas travel requires a team effort. EP staff, and especially the EP specialist assigned to provide protection for a particular trip, should develop a close working relationship with the principal's executive assistant, who is most likely the first person to learn about planned executive travel. It also pays benefits to work closely with the corporate travel department. In many organizations, even those with formal EP programs, it is the executive assistant or corporate travel department (which could be in-house or outsourced) that books commercial flights and makes lodging and ground transportation arrangements. Ideally, the EP staff would make those arrangements, but if that is not the organization's system, it is essential that EP staff at least be able to assist in such planning. Because EP specialists spend time researching conditions at the destination and know about potential threats in hotels and from car services, they should be able to influence the selection of travel dates (in case there is unrest at the destination), airlines (in case some are known to have better security than others), hotels (selected on the basis of being in a safe area and having good security and fire emergency practices), and ground transportation (so that, especially in high-risk areas, trained security drivers are used whenever possible).

Good coordination and rapport with the principal's executive assistant pays off in other ways, too. The EP specialist should ask the person to notify the EP program of major upcoming activities on the executive's schedule, such as travel or major speeches. Even if the executive prefers not to be accompanied by security staff to certain events and on certain trips, the EP program still has a responsibility to increase the principal's safety. If the principal plans to travel without security staff on a particular trip, the EP specialist can prepare an assessment of the threats faced at the destination and pass it to the principal through the executive assistant. It may also be possible to brief the executive or provide written advice on security measures for all travel modes that might be used (commercial and private planes, autos, boats, ships, and trains).

It also helps to develop a rapport with those who provide the actual transportation services. If the executive travels by corporate aircraft, the EP specialist should get to know the chief pilot and crew and share security tips with them. To the degree possible, the EP program should check out the backgrounds of any drivers who might be hired on overseas trips. If their security training is suspect, the EP specialist can at least advise them to do the following:

- Keep vehicle doors locked and windows closed.
- Avoid becoming boxed in at traffic lights.
- Avoid stopping at accident scenes. (Instead, use a mobile phone to call the police for help.)
- Be suspicious of minor, possibly deliberate rear-end collisions.
- Know evasive maneuvers.
- Keep the vehicle's speed up (minimizing the executive's exposure).
- Where possible, use the most protected lane (typically a highway's passing lane).
- Do not leave the car unattended.

The preceding advice does not substitute for genuine security driver training, but it may add a little to the driver's security capabilities. Merely talking to the driver about security sends the message that the EP operation is concerned about the principal and expects that the driver will take good care of him or her.

The EP specialist should also establish at least an introductory level of contact with emergency medical providers, such as hospitals, trauma centers, medical transportation providers, and suitable doctors in the areas to be visited.

Communication Center

Another important security measure for out-of-town travel—especially foreign travel—is to establish a 24-hour communication center. The communication center is simply a constantly staffed point of contact, such as the existing security or EP office, with which the EP specialist or the executive checks in regularly and which keeps important emergency information on hand. If the executive or EP specialist should have any minor concerns during the trip, messages can be traded through the communication center. If a large problem develops on the principal's trip, the EP specialist or the principal can call the communication center and be confident of reaching someone who can help. If, in the worst case scenario, the principal disappears, the habit of checking in frequently either by the principal or the EP specialist will mean that the communication center knows the principal's most recent whereabouts and can begin coordinating a response.

The communication center is also a useful tool for contingency planning. If, while the principal is traveling, flights are canceled or diverted, a quick call to the communication center by either the EP specialist or the principal can set in motion the process for recalculating the travel plan. For example, the EP specialist may have performed a careful advance of the destination city, the route from the airport to the hotel, the contract drivers, the hotel's security features, and appropriate and safe restaurants nearby. The EP specialist may even have flown to the destination a day ahead in order to be able to meet the principal and provide protection immediately. Then, due to weather or equipment problems, the principal's flight is diverted to another city. If he or she is the sort of principal who faces a moderate to high risk, it will not do for the principal to arrive at a strange airport, catch the first taxi in line, and stay in a hotel of unknown security qualifications. In such cases, staff at the communication center can get busy doing their research, calling their international contacts, and arranging for the principal to be transported, housed, and fed safely. They can also work on rebooking appropriate flights, rescheduling meetings, and reworking a host of security plans.

More on the Advance

This section explores several travel-related advance issues that were not addressed in Chapter 8: Know Before You Go. By performing trial runs and evaluating transportation, lodging, and the places at which the executive will conduct business, the EP specialist smooths the executive's path. The result is both safer and more convenient travel. The foreknowledge that comes from an advance allows the EP specialist to eliminate many problems and steer the protectee clear of various dangers.

What does an advance entail? For example, in performing a hotel advance, the EP specialist would visit the hotel; take photos or video footage to familiarize other security staffers with the site; meet with the manager to make special arrangements and obtain names of secondary contacts; meet with the director of security, doorman, bell captain, maître d', valet parking manager, and others; inspect the hotel's safety features; determine the range of hotel services; gather information about restaurant and recreational facilities; and determine the location and phone numbers of the nearest fire department, police department, and rescue squad. After all that, it gets worse: a thorough advance covers *two* hotels in each city to be visited—in case one suddenly becomes unavailable (due to fire) or unsuitable (due to changed conditions around the hotel, such as civic unrest).

In business travel, smooth connections, check-ins, pickups, and drop-offs can easily give the executive an extra two hours per day of work time or rest time. Travel facilitation also reduces the executive's exposure to attacks. For example, if hotel check-in, billing, luggage handling, parking, and other matters are worked out in advance, the executive can step out of the car at the hotel's front or side door, walk straight to the elevators, and arrive quickly at his or her room.

Foreign Travel Risks

The author's firm has provided protective services and consulting for principals' trips to numerous high-risk areas of the world. The risks associated with such travel are significant.[51] Dangers run high not just in war-torn areas like Afghanistan and Iraq but also in countries that are major trading partners with developed nations—in other words, places that executives might well have reason to visit.

In fact, U.S. corporations increasingly have operations in some of the world's more dangerous locales. One major, U.S.-based multinational corporation that came to R. L. Oatman & Associates for EP advice periodically sends its top executives to visit plants in Latin America. It caused the consultants great concern that some of those principals had experienced armed attacks during such trips. The occurrence of threats and harmful incidents in the past is a strong predictor of future threats and harmful incidents. To give a flavor of what can really happen, even to executives of a non-controversial company, and even when they are receiving some form of personal protection, the following are true accounts of some of their dangerous experiences:

---

[51] Travel warnings and consular information sheets from the U.S. Department of State provide updated information on risk conditions in various countries. (Much valuable travel information can be found at http://travel.state.gov.) The State Department's observations on crime conditions in many destinations that businesspeople might visit are often specific enough to guide security decisions. For example, the State Department Web site recently noted that "all areas of São Paulo have a high rate of armed robbery of pedestrians at stoplights."

- While a principal was visiting São Paolo, Brazil, the car in which he was riding was pulled over by armed men in what appeared to be a police car. The apparent attackers pointed guns at the principal's car. The security vehicle following him pulled over, and the security staff talked to the attackers and convinced them to abandon their plan. Regardless of whether the armed persons were real police, such an incident is extremely dangerous. The principal, who travels extensively, observed that such incidents are not uncommon in Brazil.

- On a recent trip to Mexico, a different principal with the same company was riding as a passenger in a Chevrolet Suburban on a toll road. At the toll booth, with the gate down, his vehicle was blocked in by a pickup truck carrying six armed men. There was much yelling and brandishing of weapons, but finally his driver calmed the situation down and the principal's car was able to leave. Nevertheless, it was clearly a very dangerous situation.

- On a recent trip to Argentina, yet another principal with the company was dismayed by the freewheeling gun handling practiced by his contract security detail. One of the guards kept his pistol unholstered and concealed under a sport coat draped over his arm, even in a crowded elevator next to the principal. The principal expressed concern, rightly, that accidental jostling in the elevator could have led to a discharge of the gun.

- One of the company's Brazilian plants received a series of telephone tips claiming that a director of the company was going to be kidnapped and used to gain access to a local plant so the payroll could be stolen. Further investigation (including involvement by the Brazilian Federal Kidnapping Squad) concluded that the calls may have been part of an attempt at drumming up business for a security provider or even local law enforcement. No particular employee was named as the target, and the caller failed to realize that payroll was not handled at that plant in a way that would make it susceptible to theft. Nevertheless, the incident shows the type of milieu into which executives may enter when they travel to Latin America.

- One of the company's longtime customers in Mexico was kidnapped. During the course of negotiations, the kidnappers delivered first his finger and then his ear.

Travel to Latin America is especially risky for a number of reasons:

- "Express kidnapping"—that is, short-term kidnapping for an amount of money that can be obtained quickly—is common in Latin America.
- Crime levels, as well as they can be ascertained, are high in many Latin American countries, for local residents as well as U.S. executives who might travel there.
- Many countries there suffer from pervasive corruption among the police and other government officials.
- There is a growth in anti-American sentiment and leftist political activism in some of the countries of Latin America.

An additional risk of international travel is this: as U.S. government installations abroad become better protected (that is, become "harder targets"), the facilities of U.S. businesses may become more attractive targets for terrorists wishing to harm U.S. interests. For example, Paul Johnson, a 49-year-old Lockheed Martin Corporation employee, was kidnapped by Islamic terrorists (members of al Qaeda) in Riyadh, Saudi Arabia, on June 12, 2004, and found decapitated six days later. Attacking a U.S. military installation or embassy is difficult; attacking U.S. businesspeople is much easier.

The State Department advises U.S. citizens and travelers to avoid visiting or lingering at "soft target" locations—in other words, locations that lack, or have less formal, security protection. Targets may include vehicles, boats, clubs, restaurants, places of worship, schools, recreational events, hotels, beaches, resorts, and areas where U.S. citizens and citizens of other Western nations are known to visit or congregate. Businesses and facilities owned or controlled by U.S. interests are also at risk.

Sooner or later, if a company continues to have close calls like those experienced by the company discussed above, the likelihood of injury to or death of a company executive is high. In fact, a member of the board of directors of that company's Central American franchisee was later murdered in El Salvador during a kidnapping attempt.

A less exotic but more likely cause of injury or death to a principal who is traveling is a hotel fire. The EP specialist can improve a principal's safety by putting together a "life bag" and ensuring that the principal brings it on the trip. The bag, kept to a compact size, should contain foreign currency, a smoke mask, duct tape, a cutting tool, directions on how to survive a hotel fire, a flashlight, extra prescription medicines and eyeglasses, emergency contact numbers (including the booklet *Key Officers of Foreign Service Posts* for U.S. government contacts overseas), and other survival items. The EP specialist should have a life bag, too, so he or she can get to the principal and provide help.

Commercial Versus Private Air Travel

Commercial air travel presents risks both on the ground and in the air. On the ground, at large, busy airports, inconvenient delays can occur during pickup and drop-off; the principals may be recognized and bothered by other travelers; airport lobbies (on the unsecured side) are notorious terrorist targets; and passing through busy security checkpoints can create opportunities for loss of personal property, missed flights, and awkward or embarrassing searches.

By contrast, private air travel is not packed with people who would bother the principal and is generally more oriented to customer service. Further, the small lobbies of general aviation FBOs (fixed-base operators) are not prime targets for terrorists who wish to draw attention to their cause. Flying via general (private) aviation reduces the likelihood of being in the wrong place at the wrong time—that is, of happening to be at a major public airport during a significant attack.

In the air, in commercial air travel, the principal has no way to know whether a dangerous person is aboard his or her plane. By contrast, in private aviation, it is likely that the principal will personally recognize every passenger on the aircraft, or at least that the passengers will be known to someone on the aircraft. No matter who principals might be targeted by, they are less likely to be accessible to adversaries if they use private aircraft.

This view is supported by a recent article in the security press:[52]

> A recent report in the Wall Street Journal was critical of the use of corporate aircraft as a security precaution, particularly for an executive's personal travel....
>
> [S]ecurity professionals responsible for executive protection defend the practice as an essential tool in securing the safety of top management as well as maintaining business efficiency....
>
> Corporate jet usage for security is a "small piece of a big security circle," said John Sullivan, director of worldwide security for Texas Instruments and head of the company's flight department. "In that circle, you've got to have a bona fide security program that shows you've got everything from alarms, a security program for the residences of your key people and that you have a protection program that covers them 24/7."
>
> The advantages of the use of corporate aircraft to a security director—and to a corporate executive—are many: flexibility

---

[52] Andrea Gural, "Corporate Jet as Security Tool: New Criticism by Shareholders, Wall Street, Raises Security Argument," *Security Director News*, November 2005, p. 1.

in flight schedules; authority over the identity of other passengers and crew; the selection of smaller, easier to secure, general aviation airports instead of large commercial hubs; and the ability to have nearly complete control over the flight's departure, flight and arrival.

"Corporate aviation's record bears out that strong security rationale," said Dan Hubbard, spokesman for the National Business Aviation Association, a trade group for the business aviation industry. "The aircrafts don't get hijacked, and no one ever snoops through or takes a bag which often contains sensitive information."...

Not only do jets function like traveling offices, with e-mail, Internet and fax capability, but they have removed many security concerns of global business expansion by allowing executives to more safely travel to foreign destinations considered Third World in infrastructure or resources.

"From a security perspective, if you are going to a Third World country, you don't have to put your top executive on a Third World airline," Sullivan said.

EP staff may be able to offer advice as to whether the principal will fly on commercial or private aircraft, but in most cases the decision will be up to the company or the principal. The EP specialist will have to do his or her best to ensure the principal's safety no matter what type of flying is chosen.

Commercial Air Travel

Commercial air travel does not provide as many opportunities for EP staff intervention as it once did. Since its formation (shortly after the September 11, 2001, terror attacks in the United States), the Transportation Security Administration (TSA) has added a host of measures to improve the security of commercial air travel. For some principals, commercial air travel still presents many risks, but they lie mainly outside the secured area of an airport, having to do with being accosted, attacked, or kidnapped in the luggage claim area or as they transition to ground transportation.

If a principal has concerns about commercial air travel, he or she is likely to ask the EP specialist for information. In fact, the

EP specialist has a duty to understand the security measures taken in commercial air travel because they affect the principal's risk level. The following are just a few of the changes to the security of commercial air travel made by TSA. Some of the measures are new, while others are upgrades of existing practices.[53]

Federal Air Marshal Service

The Federal Air Marshal Service deploys federal air marshals (FAMs) to detect, deter, and defeat hostile acts targeting U.S. air carriers, airports, passengers, and crews. FAMs are federal law enforcement officers. They attempt to blend in with passengers, and they have received training in investigative techniques, criminal terrorist behavior recognition, firearms proficiency, aircraft-specific tactics, and close-quarters self-defense measures.

The Federal Air Marshal Service began in 1968 as the Federal Aviation Administration Sky Marshal Program. In 1985, it grew into the Federal Air Marshal Service. On September 11, 2001, the Federal Air Marshal Service consisted of fewer than 50 FAMs. As a result of the 9/11 attacks, President George W. Bush ordered the rapid expansion of the service. The current number of FAMS is classified.

Federal Flight Deck Officer Program

Flight crew members are authorized to use firearms to defend against a terrorist attempt to wrest control of the aircraft. A flight crew member may be a pilot, flight engineer, or navigator assigned to the flight. If both pilots are armed, the captain decides who will defend the aircraft and who will fly it.

Under the Homeland Security Act of 2002, Congress required TSA to establish procedural requirements for an armed flight deck officer program. Now, flight crew members are trained on the use of firearms, the use of force, legal issues, defensive tactics, the

---

[53] Information based on reports at www.tsa.gov.

psychology of survival, and standard operating procedures.

Crew Member Self-Defense Training

Airlines are required to provide basic security training for all crew members. TSA is required to provide optional self-defense classes to crew members who want further training. Classes are available to all crew members who wish to take them.

TSA began nationwide deployment of the Crew Member Self-Defense Training Program in December 2004. Classes are available in 10 U.S. cities.

Security Technology Deployment

TSA has deployed a number of new technologies to detect weapons and explosives in transportation environments. The following are a few, and new technologies are developed constantly:

- **Passenger screening.** TSA has deployed 59 explosives detection trace portals, also known as "puffer" machines, at 24 airports. At the security checkpoint, puffs of air are blown at a passenger walking through a portal that looks like a familiar walk-through metal detector. The air is then analyzed for explosives.

  Passengers at several airports may undergo screening by an explosives detection document scanner. The document scanner analyzes samples collected by swiping the surface of a document over a collection disc and alerts the screener if explosive residue is detected. If the presence of explosives is indicated, the passenger is referred for additional screening. A more highly automated version of this same technology is under review by TSA.

  In addition, TSA's Transportation Security Laboratory is reviewing a technology known as backscatter. Backscatter signals interact with explosives, plastics, and metals, giving them shape and form and making them easy to interpret visually. When a passenger steps into the machine, the technology produces an outline of the passenger and allows a screener to detect any explosives, prohibited items, or weapons. Because of the detailed view of the traveler's body, privacy concerns have been raised. Still, TSA expects to begin testing the technology in the field soon.

- **Checked luggage screening.** TSA and private industry are working together on next-generation explosives detection equipment for screening checked luggage. Currently, TSA uses two types of equipment to screen checked luggage: explosives detection systems and explosives trace detection equipment.

- **Biometrics.** In summer 2006, TSA plans to launch the Registered Traveler (RT) Program nationwide. Under the RT program, passengers can volunteer to undergo a security assessment and are enrolled in the program if approved. RT users will still be required to go through primary screening at the checkpoint but, according to TSA, "will avoid additional screening at the checkpoint most of the time." At present, it is unclear how much time and inconvenience RT participants will save.

  Another program using biometrics is the Transportation Worker Identification Credential Program. In this pilot, a card that includes biometric information is used to verify the identity of individuals with access to secure areas of the nation's transportation system.

Canine and Explosives Program

The TSA National Explosives Detection Canine Program attempts to deter and detect the introduction of explosive devices into the transportation system, including swiftly resolving bomb threats. The program was formerly managed under the Federal Aviation Administration.

On March 9, 1972, a Trans World Airlines jet bound for Los Angeles took off from JFK International Airport in New York. Moments into the flight, the airline received an anonymous phone call warning there was a bomb aboard. The aircraft returned to JFK where passengers were evacuated and a bomb-sniffing dog was brought in to search. The dog found the explosive device just 12 minutes before it was set to detonate. That same day, then-President Nixon directed the Secretary of Transportation to use innovative means to combat the problems plaguing civil aviation. The result was the creation of the FAA Explosives Detection Canine Team Program, designed to place certified teams at strategic locations throughout the nation so that any aircraft receiving a bomb threat could quickly divert to an airport with a canine team.

Notification of Deficient Security

TSA provides another valuable service: notifying the public when it deems security standards to be inadequate at airports outside the United States. That information is, of course, vital to an EP specialist whose protectee may be traveling to such an airport. The following is a recent TSA press release making such a notification:[54]

> The Transportation Security Administration (TSA) today announced that the Bandara Ngurah Rai International Airport in Bali, Indonesia does not meet international security standards, and the department is taking action to warn travelers of this security deficiency. Based on an assessment by a team of security experts from TSA, the Department of Homeland Security has determined that the airport does not currently maintain security measures consistent with the standards established by the International Civil Aviation Organization (ICAO).
>
> In view of this finding, Homeland Security has directed air carriers issuing tickets for travel between the United States

[54] Transportation Security Administration, "TSA Finds Security at Bandara Ngurah Rai International Airport Does Not Meet International Standards," press release, December 23, 2005.

and Indonesia to notify ticket purchasers of the identity of this airport in accordance with this determination. Homeland Security also directed that the identity of this airport be displayed prominently at all U.S. airports and published in the Federal Register....

TSA representatives have been in Indonesia to help airport authorities bring Bandara Ngurah Rai International Airport up to international standards. The TSA representatives will continue to work with Indonesia and to assist local authorities with correcting security deficiencies at the airport as quickly as possible.

U.S. and foreign air carriers that fly directly between the United States and Indonesia are temporarily providing additional security measures that counter the deficiencies identified at the airport. If proper precautions are carefully observed by both the air carriers and the airport, Homeland Security believes that it is possible to safely conduct air service operations to and from Bandara Ngurah Rai International Airport.

Another new TSA program, the Armed Security Officer Program, is described below in the private flight operations section, as it applies only to private or general aviation.

Despite all the foregoing measures, many security experts believe an attack against a commercial aircraft could still happen. However, 100 percent security is an impossible goal. At the very least, it seems that the measures discussed are likely to improve the security of commercial air travel.

Private Flight Operations

Many corporations and wealthy families are turning to private air travel, either by purchasing aircraft outright or by participating in fractional ownership arrangements. The benefits of private air travel (also called general aviation or GA in some publications) include both convenience and security. When one flies commercially, the major security measures are taken by TSA, the airport, or the airline. When one engages in private air travel, a greater responsibility for security falls on the EP specialist, as well as corporate flight crew and fixed-base operator (FBO) staff.

EP operations have long considered private air travel to be potentially more secure. In commercial air travel, there is no way for an EP specialist to search the luggage of other passengers, and when traveling commercially, the principal is surrounded by unknown persons whose motives are equally unknown. By contrast, in private travel, the EP operation can inspect any item it wants to inspect and can ensure that no unknown persons board the aircraft. In addition, terrorist hijackings up to now have tended to focus on large, commercial aircraft, though some small planes have been used (but not hijacked) for attacks. A downside of general aviation is that the smaller airports that private aircraft often use tend to have less rigorous security of their grounds and hangars.

The tactics of terrorists and other criminals change regularly in response to security measures, among other factors. Thus, the relative advantages and disadvantages of commercial and private travel may shift over time. On April 20, 2006, the Transportation Security Administration released the following advisory:[55]

> On April 13, 2006, a message posted in Arabic on a web forum explained how to identify private American jets and urged Muslims to destroy all such aircraft:

> "Destroy private American aircraft…. We call upon all Muslims to follow and identify private civilian American aircrafts in all airports of the world…. It is the duty of Muslims to destroy all types of private American aircrafts that are of the types Gulf Stream and Lear Jet and all small jet aircraft usually used by distinguished (people) and businessmen."

> TSA reminds general aviation aircraft and airport owners and operators to review the security measures contained in the TSA Information Publication, *Security Guidelines for General Aviation Airports,* and the Aircraft Owners and Pilots Association's Airport Watch Program materials.

---

[55] Transportation Security Administration, "Advisory—Security Information for Aircraft Owners/Operators & Airport Managers," April 20, 2006.

In addition, general aviation aircraft and airport owners and operators are encouraged to consider the following:

- Secure unattended aircraft to prevent unauthorized use.

- Verify the identification of crew and passengers prior to departure.

- Verify that baggage and cargo are known to the persons on board.

- Where identification systems are in place, encourage employees to wear proper identification and challenge persons not wearing proper identification.

- Direct increased vigilance to unknown pilots and/or clients for aircraft rental or charters—as well as unknown service/delivery personnel.

- Be alert/aware of and report persons masquerading as pilots, security personnel, emergency medical technicians, or other personnel using uniforms and/or vehicles as methods to gain access to aviation facilities or aircraft.

- Be alert/aware of and report aircraft with unusual or unauthorized modifications.

- Be alert/aware of and report persons loitering in the vicinity of aircraft or air operations areas — as well as persons loading unusual or unauthorized payload onto aircraft.

- Be alert/aware of and report persons who appear to be under stress or the control of other persons.

- Be alert/aware of and report persons whose identification appears altered or inconsistent.

The theft of any General Aviation aircraft should be immediately reported to the appropriate authorities and the TSA General Aviation Hotline at (866) 427-3287. In addition, persons should report any suspicious activity immediately to local law enforcement.

Many persons receiving executive protection fly often or only on private aircraft. Thus, the remaining sections in this chapter discuss procedures for increasing the security for private air travel.

Risk Assessment

The first step in developing a corporate aircraft security plan is to assess the risk level. Any corporate air fleet faces a certain base risk level, which pertains generally to theft and vandalism. Another category of risk depends on the particular executives or company associated with the aircraft. The aircraft could be targeted if the corporation is involved in controversial activities, if the executives maintain a high profile, or if aircraft travels to high-crime countries.

The factors that bring risk to aircraft and passengers change continually. Thus, the EP specialist may need to alter the assessment of the risk level at any time, based on current information. For instance, shortly after the September 11, 2001, terrorist attacks, one company the author advises developed reliable intelligence that its aircraft and passengers faced an elevated risk. To deal with that increased threat, the company established a practice of sending an EP specialist on every corporate flight. The EP specialist not only provided security during flights but also was responsible for ensuring physical and procedural security of aircraft on the ground.

Other factors may also affect the risk assessment. For example, in fractional ownership arrangements, a company might own a one-quarter share of a certain type and size of aircraft. However, the company will not always be assigned the same type of aircraft. The aircraft management company may on occasion supply different but comparable models. The security staff should therefore be prepared to secure not only the type of aircraft that the company bought fractionally but also all aircraft that could be substituted for it.

Information Gathering

If something goes wrong before, during, or after a corporate flight, the EP specialist could be the first person called. To be able to respond to questions and crises effectively, he or she should obtain the following details before a flight:

- aircraft's year, make, tail number, and hours of flight time
- fuel range and luggage and passenger capacity
- number of flight attendants on the aircraft, if any
- aircraft's interior layout and facilities
- names and phone numbers of the chief pilot and copilot
- destination airport's name, address, phone number, and hours of operation
- destination airport's runway length and restrictions on night landings, noise, and type of aircraft
- availability of mechanics, fuel, de-icing equipment, security, and catering
- police jurisdiction in which the airport resides
- average ambulance response time and nearest hospital with a trauma unit
- alternative arrival sites in case of bad weather, as well as ground transportation options from those sites

Physical Security

To whatever extent private air travel is more secure than commercial air travel, it is due to the efforts of corporate security and EP staff—specifically, the control they can exert over the physical environment and the passenger list. It is not because of any intrinsic security advantage on the part of small airports or the fixed-based operators (FBOs) that run facilities there. Corporate aircraft can fly into approximately 5,400 U.S. public-use airports, compared with about 580 airports served by scheduled air carriers. The public-use airports are owned by local municipalities, usually without much funding or expertise to devote to security. Thus, corporate aircraft frequently travel to small—and possibly less secure—airports.

However, the EP specialist and, if applicable, corporate flight program can take steps to increase the level of security surrounding their own operation. From good luggage control to protecting the aircraft when it is left unattended, the EP program can set the desired standard of security.

The Congressional Research Service (CRS), a branch of the Library of Congress, is the public policy research arm of the United States Congress. CRS recently issued a report on physical security measures for general aviation airports. The following are highlights:[56]

> Other than surveillance, access controls, and background checks, there are a variety of other options for enhancing the general physical security of airport facilities. One of the most obvious…is erecting physical barriers, such as chain-link perimeter fencing, around security sensitive locations on the airfield. However, the TSA cautions that while physical barriers such as fencing, walls, electronic boundaries, and even natural barriers can protect airport areas from unauthorized access, these methods by themselves will not prevent determined intruders from gaining access…. Besides fencing, protective lighting can often serve as an effective deterrent against theft, vandalism, unauthorized access, and other illegal activity at night.
>
> …[T]he TSA notes that storing aircraft in hangars provides one of the most effective method of securing GA [general aviation] aircraft. However, at many GA airports, hangar space is in short supply and the demand for hangars makes them very costly….
>
> While surveillance, access controls, and physical security measures at airports can provide effective deterrents, these measures may be costly and challenging to implement at many GA airports, especially smaller airports….
>
> The TSA's *Security Guidelines for General Aviation Airports* recommends storing aircraft in locked hangars, consistent use of aircraft door locks, using keyed ignitions when appropriate, and not leaving keys in aircraft as some basic steps to secure GA aircraft. The guidelines also recommend using an auxiliary lock such as commercially available propeller, throttle, or

---

[56] Bart Elias, "Securing General Aviation," a Congressional Research Service Report for Congress, December 15, 2005. Accessed May 1, 2006, at http://opencrs.cdt.org/getfile.php?rid=44397.

tie down locks to further protect GA aircraft. The TSA suggests that "[p]ilots should employ multiple methods of securing their aircraft to make it as difficult as possible for an unauthorized person to gain access to it." However, it is apparent that this common sense advice is not always heeded. In the October 2005 theft of a Cessna Citation VII business jet, it was reported that the aircraft—which does not need a key to start—was left unlocked.

While building or renting secured hangar space may be cost prohibitive to many light aircraft owners, locks and other security devices may provide a common sense, cost effective means to reduce the vulnerability of GA aircraft to theft. Given that aircraft are high value assets, locks may offer a relatively low-cost means to reduce vulnerability. Purchasing and installing secondary locks could benefit aircraft owners and operators by providing added protection against theft and unauthorized access.

In the absence of explicit federal standards or requirements, some states have taken initiatives to require specific actions for securing GA aircraft. New Jersey, for example, has implemented a state-wide "two-lock rule" requiring any aircraft parked or stored at a GA facility within the state for more than 24 hours to either secure the aircraft with two distinct locking devices or disable the aircraft in a manner to prevent theft or illegal use. The Strengthen Aviation Security Act (H.R. 2649) would require airport operators to ensure that "...all general aviation aircraft, while parked at such airports, are secured by a visible immobilizing device (such as a prop lock)." Propeller locks and throttle locks may provide relatively low cost, relatively effective deterrents to unauthorized use and theft of aircraft.

The preceding recommendations make sense. Employing the concept of rings of security, the outer ring consists of perimeter defense (such as a chain-link fence, gated checkpoints, well-secured hangars, and even the use of a portable microwave fence kit).[57] The inner ring consists of locking and alarm mechanisms on the aircraft itself, procedures controlling who may enter the air-

---

[57] Such a kit uses four sets of transmitters and receivers to create an invisible fence around the aircraft. If the signal along any side is interrupted, the system generates an alarm.

port's restricted area or the aircraft itself, luggage screening, the use of security officers to protect the aircraft, and other such measures. The job of the EP program is to ensure that the aircraft receives effective security when it is at its home airport, when it is aloft, and when it reaches (and waits at) its destination.

The aircraft should be parked in a locked or guarded hangar whenever possible, and access control and intrusion detection devices should be used in the hangar. When the plane is kept away from its home base, it typically will not have access to a hangar. The assistance of local security service providers may be needed to bolster other physical protection measures.

As for the aircraft itself, the EP manager should request that the locks originally installed on the aircraft be replaced with high-quality, professionally installed locks because of the widespread unauthorized possession of master keys to manufacturer-installed locks and the possibility of loss of key control over time. Keys to the aircraft should not be left with the airport operator unless EP staff can verify that the keys will be secured and controlled. As an added safety measure, the aircraft should not display the corporate logo or other identifying marks.

While the plane is on the ground, it should always be locked when unattended, parked away from perimeter gates and fences, and located in a well-lit area. If the plane is to remain for an extended period, a member of the flight crew should visit the aircraft at least once a day to inspect it, ensure that it is properly secured, and search for signs of tampering.

The various physical security measures described above and below may be carried out by the EP specialists. However, it is more likely they will be requested and possibly confirmed by the EP specialist but carried out by the flight crew, corporate security department, or staff of a flight center operated by the principal's corporation. Aside from the measures already mentioned, other physical measures for securing the aircraft fall into three categories:

- **Intrusion detection.** To prevent unauthorized persons from gaining access to the aircraft, flight operations staff can use seals on cabin and luggage doors or an electronic detection system designed specifically for aircraft. When leaving the aircraft, the pilot or another flight crew member can arm the system, which will then monitor the main cabin door, the emergency exits, the fuel door, and any other doors or panels that provide access to the cabin (recording the date, time, and duration of each opening). On returning to the aircraft, the pilot or crew member can check the system's status to determine whether any tampering attempts were made.

  In addition, authorized personnel can employ a handheld transceiver to query the aircraft intrusion system from a distance to ascertain the time and date of all legitimate entries and the identities of those entering. If illegitimate entries have been made or attempted, the device will report their location. The system is also capable of transmitting an alarm by radio.

  Another option is to install a simple door counter, which counts the number of times a door has been opened. Personnel can determine whether the aircraft was entered by checking whether the counter reading is higher than it was when the plane was secured.

- **Removable materials.** Regarding the contents of the aircraft, all removable materials should be marked by engraving, color striping, or both. Such identification will help flight staff notice if an item has been removed and replaced with another, perhaps dangerous, item.

- **Preflight inspection.** Planes have a number of vulnerable external areas where explosives could be placed, such as wheel wells that can be accessed when the plane is parked unattended either in a hangar or on the tarmac. Pi-

lots or the flight crew should conduct a thorough preflight inspection of the aircraft, including every access
panel and vent, to ensure that the aircraft has not been
tampered with.

Procedural Measures

In addition to the physical security measures already described, the
flight operation should employ a variety of procedures to observe
the aircraft and manage staff, passengers, and luggage. The following are some of the most important of those procedures:

- **General surveillance.** Airport and aircraft personnel
  should be asked to watch the perimeter, the hangar, and
  any public areas for any person who may be paying undue
  attention to the grounds or the aircraft, including video-
  taping the site. If specific threat information is received,
  EP or corporate security personnel may need to set up
  countersurveillance.

- **Staff.** Flight operations staff should verify the identities of
  anyone performing maintenance or repair work on the
  aircraft. In addition, a member of the flight crew should
  oversee the fueling process to prevent any harmful behavior by an adversary.

  Airport employee parking should be separate from
  visitor parking. Such an arrangement makes it more difficult for an adversary to blend in with employees coming
  from the parking lot and perhaps enter restricted areas
  through an entrance that is not properly controlled.

- **Passengers**. Fortunately, the number of persons that will
  board a corporate plane is small, but passenger security
  must still be strict. Passengers should be asked to wait in a
  designated lounge until boarding is announced. They
  should not be permitted in the hangar area or in the immediate ramp area where the aircraft is readied for flight

unless they are escorted. Airport and corporate security staff should challenge all unauthorized people and immediately report any suspicious persons to law enforcement.

To ensure that only authorized guests enter the plane, security should insist that the crew be given a passenger manifest before the flight. A member of the flight crew should meet with and verify the identity of each passenger on the manifest before allowing that passenger to board. If the lead passenger (typically, the executive in charge of the trip) is not there or cannot personally identify a passenger, the flight crew member should require that passenger to display a photo ID. During threat alerts, some corporations go so far as to declare that only company employees can travel on the corporate aircraft.

To ensure that passengers can get proper medical care if they become ill, they should complete medical profile cards. Passengers retain the cards to preserve their medical privacy, but the flight crew can access this key medical information in an emergency. As has been stated before, executive protection extends beyond protecting principals from deliberate attacks by adversaries; it also calls for safeguarding principals from or quickly responding to accidents, medical emergencies, fires, and other hazards.

- **Luggage.** Strict luggage control is essential—even in the seemingly less formal atmosphere of corporate aviation. It should include asking passengers whether someone else packed their bags, whether their bags were unattended at any time since being packed, and whether they were asked to carry anything on board for someone else.

  If the answer to any of those questions is yes, or if the traveler seems uncertain, flight operations staff should ask for permission to conduct a discreet physical search of the bags. Afterward, colored tags should be attached to the luggage to show that it has been inspected.

The unpredictable nature of the current war against terrorism leads to some uncertainties in corporate aviation. The possibility of temporary closure of some airports to corporate aircraft (in response to the terrorist threat) means that the EP and flight operations staff must prepare several backup plans. They may have to research the security of, and safe transport to and from, alternative airports. If the airport that the company is accustomed to using becomes unavailable suddenly, security should know which nearby airports can provide adequate security.

Other Protective Capabilities

The protective objective is to prevent security incidents, but sometimes they happen despite one's best efforts. Therefore, the EP specialist and flight crew must be prepared to respond in case an adversary succeeds in boarding the plane or placing a hazardous item on board. They should work together to develop a response plan.

First and foremost are training and awareness. Everyone who will play a role in any incident plans should go over them beforehand in tabletop exercises to practice their roles. Once the aircraft's engines are started, the flight crew should be suspicious of any attempts to delay, stop, or otherwise impede departure, unless those attempts come from air traffic control authorities.

In addition, for the times when they will fly aboard private aircraft, EP specialists should familiarize themselves with in-flight emergency procedures and the location of fire extinguishers, emergency flotation vests, and life rafts. With that information, the EP specialist becomes a security resource for the flight crew. The EP specialist should be the last person on board before takeoff and the first out the door upon landing to ensure that the aircraft is safe.

Another type of training that EP specialists may want to obtain for themselves and even, possibly, for their principals, is basic flight training for use in an emergency. For example, the Aircraft Owners and Pilots Association (AOPA), based in Frederick, Maryland, offers a "pinch hitter" course designed to enable the student to land a small plane in an emergency if the pilot becomes incapacitated.

The TSA recently developed a new and unusual program for boosting security on general aviation flights to and from Ronald Reagan Washington National Airport (DCA). The program calls for training and authorization of armed security officers to ride as passengers on such flights. The following provides highlights of the program:[58]

> The Transportation Security Administration (TSA), in coordination with the Federal Air Marshal Service (FAMS), announces implementation of the Armed Security Officer (ASO) Program. The ASO Program will enable interested persons who meet eligibility requirements and have qualifying law enforcement experience to provide armed security aboard General Aviation (GA) aircraft authorized to operate into and out of Ronald Reagan Washington National Airport (DCA), starting in October 2005.
>
> An Interim Final Rule (IFR) published by TSA in the Federal Register on July 15, 2005, established security procedures that will allow GA operations to resume at DCA, while protecting critical national assets from possible airborne terrorist attack. These procedures include a requirement that every GA flight operating into or out of DCA have onboard an armed security officer specially trained and authorized by TSA. Persons authorized as ASOs are not employed by the Federal government, but are compensated for their services by either a Fixed Base Operator...or the aircraft operator conducting the flight.

---

[58] Transportation Security Administration, "Transportation Security Administration Announces Armed Security Officer (ASO) Program," press release, 2005 (no date on publication). More information on the program is available through the Security & Law Enforcement link at www.tsa.gov.

Eligibility requirements include, but are not limited to, having qualifying law enforcement experience as either an active Law Enforcement Officer (LEO) in good standing; a qualified retired LEO in good standing; or a qualified former LEO in good standing with a minimum of four (4) years law enforcement experience as defined by TSA. Applicants who meet all eligibility requirements and who pass all necessary background checks must successfully complete, at their own expense, a two-day training program conducted by the FAMS at field offices located throughout the United States. Active LEOs must provide a letter from their department authorizing their participation in the program, and indicating whether they may use their department-issued firearm.

Relationship Building

EP specialists should strive to develop good working relationships with various players in the flight operations process. In many ways, secure executive travel depends on the strength of those relationships.

It is important to establish good relations with the chief pilot, flight crew, and aircraft maintenance personnel, as they will be carrying out the dictated security measures and need to know that they have the authority and the organizational support to do so. They must feel confident, for example, that they will be supported if they deny entry to any persons or refuse to allow certain items onto the aircraft.

At a company the author advises, the executive protection staff took an inclusive approach to developing the corporate aircraft security plan. The EP specialists convened a meeting with the company's chief pilot, his crew, and the mechanics working for the aircraft maintenance contractor. In the meeting, the participants discussed risks and developed a comprehensive and feasible security plan.

The team approach led to a program with maximum collaboration and minimal conflict. It also helped the EP staff become aware of risks that they might not have known about otherwise, such as contaminated fuel or an in-flight medical emergency.

An EP specialist can use his or her good relationship with the corporate aviation staff to raise their level of security awareness. All personnel involved in corporate flight operations should be treated as a part of the EP team.

Another important set of relationships involves the various destinations to which the corporate aircraft flies. For example, by getting to know local airport personnel and explaining the company's particular security needs, one company the author advises was able to obtain a more desirable aircraft parking location (closer to the main airport building and under better lighting). The EP specialist was also able to arrange for extra automobile parking in a close-in, guarded lot. That arrangement provides his company with a safe staging area and helps maintain the security of the vehicles that corporate aircraft passengers will use for ground transportation.

If the aircraft routinely travels to small, private airports that lack sophisticated security capabilities, the EP specialist should also develop relationships with local personnel who could be employed to provide on-site security.

Relationship building leads to teamwork and a sense of professional camaraderie. When more people work together to protect the principal, there are more eyes on the lookout for security risks. Having a security team that extends beyond the formal security and EP departments strengthens the concentric rings of protection around the principal.

11.
Training and Certification

General Importance of Training

In many occupations, practitioners are required to participate in continuing education regularly—from the time they finish their original training until the day they retire. In the field of executive protection, no central, national body certifies EP specialists or dictates an authorized curriculum. But even without an organized, accepted, and required path of certification and training, EP specialists owe it to themselves and their clients to get the best training they can and keep their knowledge and skills up to date.

A person contemplating a move into EP work may believe a prior career in policing provides a sufficient background for executive protection. It is a fine and helpful background, full of skills that will be essential in EP work. However, the author knows well that 20 years of law enforcement experience does not equal expertise in private sector security. The same holds true for persons coming out of military and government careers. Certification and training are key steps on the path to understanding civilian protection in the business world.

Why train? Why learn? Because the adversary does. Security is a discipline with a structure and principles that can be learned and applied to meet a variety of threatening scenarios. Physical attack, cyber terror, theft, and property damage are all threats against a principal. Many of those threats require planning, research, and discipline. Security efforts do, too. What is required is not merely good protection but ever-increasingly good protection. As EP specialists harden their principals' defenses, adversaries adapt. It is the EP specialist's responsibility to be proactive and stay one step ahead. Training is the best way to keep the balance tipped in the EP specialist's favor. Through training, practitioners can learn about the latest and best technology, techniques, and tactics.

An EP specialist could foresee many different career paths: to continue to perform well in his or her current job, to rise in the ranks, or to find a new job or new clients. In all those cases, training is essential. EP staff may find it hard to fit training into their busy schedules, but they should find the time—they may actually gain time if the training leads to time-saving procedures.

In addition, training offers more than knowledge. It also offers a chance to network and draw from others' experiences. The best piece of advice an EP specialist might hear during training could come from the peer sitting in the next chair. Part of the energizing benefit of training is found in the relationships formed during training sessions.

Training Schools

While security certification is useful, EP training is essential. Most EP specialists learn their craft through a comprehensive EP training program. In addition, some pursue EP driver training. Both categories of training are discussed below.

Comprehensive EP Training

Military, law enforcement, or corporate security experience is a common, helpful background for the practice of executive protection. In the foreground, however, should be high-quality, comprehensive training directed specifically toward private-sector EP.

Before spending the money to attend such training, the student should exercise due diligence, examining the program's faculty-to-student ratio, licensing within the program's home state, and focus on the type of EP work the student actually does or hopes to do. If the training focuses on high-threat, high-profile, gun-ready protective work (such as may be done in, for example, Bogota, Colombia, or Baghdad, Iraq), it may not be sufficiently relevant to EP in the usual corporate setting, where one cannot drive a Humvee through red lights while clutching a fully automatic weapon. Instead, the student should seek out a course that teaches how to provide quiet, behind-the-scenes protection in less dangerous areas.

One of the best-respected comprehensive executive protection training programs is the Oatman School of Executive Protection (www.rloatman.com). Since 1995 it has graduated nearly 800 people from its rigorous seven-day program in Towson, Maryland, and countless others from its traveling two-day programs (many of which are sponsored by ASIS International).

The demanding curriculum provides a solid grounding in protection fundamentals, beginning with the underlying theories that drive modern EP tactics and strategies. Mastery of the fundamentals is followed by hands-on practice in operational elements, encouraging students to think and react appropriately to the challenges of the protective environment. The goal is to provide a high standard of training for individuals who are currently involved in or who wish to enter the field of executive protection.

Students study protective theory and its application, advance work, identifying adversaries through various characteristics,[59] workplace violence, protective choreography, defensive driving, explosive detection, the use of firearms in protective assignments, and many other topics. Seven days are required to impart the full program, which consists of more than 75 hours of instruction. Class size is limited to 34 students to create good conditions for faculty–student interaction and individualized attention. The following are the major segments of the Oatman School's seven-day program:

- **Executive protection orientation.** This segment introduces students to the art of executive protection and differentiates an EP specialist from a bodyguard.

- **Threat assessment.** In this segment, students learn that threat assessment is the proper foundation of all protection programs. They learn how to gather and analyze intelligence to establish a framework for the protective effort.

- **Advance procedures.** In executive protection, it is essential to conduct advance visits to the principal's destinations and conduct advance research into all the details of those destinations (as was discussed in Chapter 8: Know Before You Go). Students learn how to conduct an advance survey of routes, airports, hotels, restaurants, and all the details that affect the trip and the stay.

- **Choreography of protection.** This segment teaches the proper physical positioning required to support the concentric theory of protection. In other words, students

---

[59] Using, for example, insights from the U.S. Secret Service Exceptional Case Study Project, as described in Robert A. Fein and Bryan Vossekuil, *Protective Intelligence & Threat Assessment Investigations: A Guide for State and Local Law Enforcement Officials* (Washington: National Institute of Justice, 2000).

learn where to stand and how closely to accompany the principal in various protective settings.

- **Countersurveillance.** Here students learn the various techniques used in "watching the watchers" (as described in this book's Chapter 5: Countersurveillance).

- **Proper dress and etiquette.** Many EP specialists come from careers in which they mainly wore uniforms to work. This segment provides guidance on how to dress appropriately for the workday and after-hours activities. The information is not obvious, as many principals inhabit circles that may be unfamiliar to the average security or law enforcement professional. Also discussed are teamwork, attitude, and working relationships in executive protection.

- **Transportation security.** This segment provides guidance on selecting the right vehicle for EP work, as well as securing it from harm and searching the vehicle for signs of tampering (including the planting of an explosive device). Also discussed are the strengths, limitations, and classifications of bullet-resistant vehicles.

- **Driving dynamics.** Students receive classroom instruction in vehicle dynamics, including accelerating, steering, stopping, sliding, and maintaining control in difficult situations. The next day, students spend the entire time in a vehicle. The emphasis is on keeping the vehicle on the pavement, practicing controlled breaking, and swerving to avoid accidents. Instructors set up 3 inch traffic cones and time students as they drive the course at assigned speeds while keeping control over the car. Students also practice threshold breaking exercises and then progress to swerving to avoid a vehicle coming into their lane. The instruction focuses on conducting those maneuvers while also transporting a principal.

- **Working executive protection in other countries.** The degree and style of executive protection that should be provided varies by principal, work locations, and travel destinations. This segment focuses particularly on providing EP throughout the world, in much of which general crime and kidnapping rates run high. Students also learn how to select the right security contractor and understand in-country cultural and language challenges.

- **Domestic and international travel.** Students learn how to develop a network of contacts and nurture their resources to assure continuity of the protective effort outside the corporate home base. Considerations include health concerns, facilitation, communication, and privacy.

- **The lone gunman.** This segment examines the thinking and behavior of individuals who have attacked or approached prominent public officials or other figures in the United States. Students also learn strategies to prevent acts of violence against a principal by understanding the behavior of attackers.

Numerous subtopics are covered within those major segments, including the following:

- emergency and evasive vehicle operation and security
- use of firearms in protective assignments
- self-defense
- open-source intelligence collection
- step-down weapons
- emergency medicine
- legal considerations
- psychological analysis of threat potential
- commercial versus private air travel

Not only do students learn a tremendous amount about executive protection, but they develop close ties with their cohort of 33 other students, who may serve as useful contacts and resources in the future. In addition, the seven-day program is certified by the Maryland Police Training Commission. Law enforcement officers from Maryland who attend the course receive in-service training hours recognized by their agency. Law enforcement attendees from other states have contacted the Maryland Police Training Commission and been granted earned in-service training credit. Students who attend the program receive four continuing education credits from ASIS International. Those credits count toward maintaining Certified Protection Professional status.

EP Driver Training

Most adults know how to drive, but only those who have received specialized executive protection driving training are likely to possess all the skills and habits needed for transporting a principal safely and professionally. EP specialists—and, when feasible, the drivers they use for executive transportation—should take initial and recurring training in EP driving.

Several firms in the United States offer such training. Among the better known are BSR (www.bsr-inc.com) and programs associated with well-known driving expert Tony Scotti (Vehicle Dynamics Institute, www.vehicledynamics.net, and Crossroads Training Academy, www.crossroadstrng.com).[60] Their programs provide both classroom instruction and driving practice on closed roads.

For example, BSR, a driving school based in Summit Point, West Virginia, offers a three-and-a-half day course in executive security training. The course is designed for "individuals who might come under a terrorist or criminal attack while operating an automobile," and it is recommended for security personnel, executives, and their drivers.

The course's key features and subjects are as follows:

---

[60] A wealth of security driving information is available at Tony Scotti's site, www.securitydriver.com.

- high-speed driving techniques

- forward and reverse ramming

- situational exercises simulating vehicular attacks

- evasive maneuvers—forward 180-degree turns (bootlegs) and reverse 180 degree turns (J-turns)

- exercises in which a student learns to prevents his or her automobile from being run off the road and stopped

- analysis of terrorist and criminal attacks

- car shoot demonstration

- evacuation drills

- searching an automobile for explosives

- route analysis and surveillance detection—practical exercises in which students conduct a route analysis, drive their routes, and attempt to detect surveillance

The first day focuses on surveillance detection. The second day provides advanced driver training, which teaches the student how to be a better, more confident driver. The third day presents BSR's evasive driving module. On the fourth day, students choose from the following:

- **Personal protection module.** Students learn about explosive devices, how to search an automobile for them, how much protection an average automobile can provide from weapons fire, and ways to evacuate an automobile that is disabled and under attack.

- **Protective detail module.** This module is designed for students who may work as part of a protective detail or in a motorcade. The training concentrates on driving at above-highway speeds on real roads, motorcade tactics, and evasive drills. The training ends with an exercise where the students work together in a motorcade that comes under attack.

- **Commandeering module.** This module, for U.S. government personnel only, would not apply to most EP specialists in the corporate environment, but it teaches how to acquire a vehicle to escape from hostile territory.

Certifications

EP-Specific

People entering the EP field often ask whether they will be officially certified in executive protection if they obtain a particular diploma or complete a particular course. At present, there is no recognized, authoritative, national EP credential in the private sector. Various training programs provide certificates, but they are in effect certificates of completion of a particular program, not certifications that have met the standards of a professional review board. However, the field is maturing (e.g., the industry standard ASIS International *Protection of Assets Manual* now contains a chapter on executive protection, written by this author), and over time a widely accepted, authoritative EP credential may be developed.

Meanwhile, every state has different regulations for EP specialists. Some do not regulate the occupation at all, while others require licensing similar to that required for investigators or security guards.

Major Security Certifications

Since there are no obvious degrees or certifications to obtain in the field of executive protection, many EP specialists opt for a more generalized security certification. The Certified Protection Professional (CPP) designation from ASIS International (formerly the American Society for Industrial Security) is by far the best-known, most widely accepted, and most authoritative general certification in the private security field. Other organizations offer certifications in security specialties like fraud examination, security consulting, and information security, but for the most part those are not directly applicable to executive protection.

In a nutshell, certification makes one a more desirable employee and job candidate. Certifications like those from ASIS serve as a screening tool to help others judge the professionalism of a given EP specialist. Moreover, because they typically have continuing education requirements, they show that the certification holder has been keeping up with the field.

The CPP designation is not a requirement for executive protection work, but the process of studying for it can provide EP specialists with a general overview of corporate security—a body of knowledge that they might lack if they come from a law enforcement or military background. Understanding corporate security and the ways in which it differs from government security is crucial to running a well-regarded, effective corporate EP program.

ASIS currently offers three certifications: Certified Protection Professional (CPP), Professional Certified Investigator (PCI), and Physical Security Professional (PSP). The first, CPP, applies to overall corporate security and helps EP specialists understand the context in which they will likely be working. PCI and PSP, though more specialized, would be worth undertaking if the EP specialist conducts or supervises investigations or oversees physical security systems.

Certified Protection Professional

Approximately 10,000 persons have earned the CPP designation since it was introduced in 1977. The CPP exam consists of 200 multiple-choice questions from eight broad subject areas:

- security principles and practices
- business principles and practices
- personnel security
- physical security
- information security
- emergency practices

- investigations
- legal aspects

Numerous organizations offer training in corporate security and executive protection, but the options for actual certification are few. If an EP specialist plans to work in the corporate environment and desires a certification to prove his or her knowledge, the CPP designation is the one to get.

Professional Certified Investigator

A relatively new designation, the PCI was introduced in 2002. The PCI exam consists of multiple-choice questions on the following topics:

- case management
- evidence collection
- case presentation

Even if investigation is not an EP specialist's primary function, the need for investigation arises often enough (e.g., background investigations or threat investigation) that the certification is worth considering.

Physical Security Professional

Like the PCI, the PSP was introduced in 2002. It is designed for people who conduct physical security surveys, design integrated security systems, or install, operate, or maintain those systems. While a deep knowledge of alarm systems is not a central requirement for EP specialists, they often have to recommend and oversee security systems for their principals' homes and offices, so a good understanding of physical security considerations is useful.

The multiple-choice PCP exam covers the following:

- physical security assessment
- selection of integrated physical security measures
- implementation of physical security measures

12.
Managing and Directing an EP Detail

Most ongoing EP operations consist of not just one but a team of EP specialists. Naturally, an EP team requires management and direction—in other words, leadership. What makes an EP manager a good leader?

With its 24-hour operations, unpredictable conditions, multiplicity of details, and life-and-death stakes, executive protection shares some characteristics with the military profession. Thus, it is relevant to look to the military's many studies of leadership. The Army War College recently published a study of leadership qualities among Army generals. *Leadership Lessons at Division Command*

Level—2004[61] reports the findings of a study that surveyed members of four Army divisions that had spent 12 to 15 months serving in Operation Iraqi Freedom. The intent was to identify "those behaviors that are crucial for contemporary leader effectiveness."

The study determined that interpersonal skills are more critical to good leadership than technical know-how. Below is the study's top 12 list of the most critical leadership behaviors. A good leader does the following:

- keeps cool under pressure
- clearly explains missions, standards, and priorities
- sees the big picture; provides context and perspective
- can make tough, sound decisions on time
- adapts quickly to new situations and requirements
- sets high standards without a "zero defects" mentality
- can handle bad news
- coaches and gives useful feedback to subordinates
- sets a high ethical tone; demands honest reporting
- knows how to delegate and not micromanage
- builds and supports teamwork within staff and among units
- is positive, encouraging, and realistically optimistic

Related to leadership is another key skill, administrative ability. Much has been written about the most visible and exciting aspect of executive protection—operations. However, little has been published about the administration of a corporate executive protection program and the complex maneuvering necessary to succeed in a highly charged, intensely competitive corporate environment. This chapter provides insights into the experience of

---

[61] The report was authored by Walter F. Ulmer, Jr., Michael D. Shaler, R. Craig Bullis, Diane F. DiClemente, and T. Owen Jacobs and is available at http://handle.dtic.mil/100.2/ADA435928 or through the National Technical Information Service.

administering the EP operation of a large corporation and draws hard-earned lessons from that experience.

The scenario presented in this chapter is that of creating an EP program where one never existed before. Establishing a protection program from scratch presents a rare but grand opportunity. It is a chance to create a custom-tailored, dynamic, and vital program. The task of building a new EP program requires corporate survival skills that may seem unrelated to those of an EP specialist but are actually necessary for the protection of a company's most valuable human asset—its top personnel.

Risk Assessment

The first steps in creating a protection program are to examine the threat environment and develop a realistic risk assessment. An EP manager cannot justify or design the program without determining the nature of the threat. He or she must consider the total protective environment—corporate and private—of the principal and, if necessary, the principal's family.

A fuller discussion of risk assessment was presented in Chapter 3, but in a nutshell, the EP manager should conduct incisive, informed, and realistic examinations of risk particular to the principal as well as general risk factors that everyone faces. This is a time to be thorough but reasonable. For example, it does not make sense to greatly emphasize the threat of terrorism against the principal unless reality makes such a confrontation probable based on who the principal is, what line of work the corporation is in, and where and how often the principal travels. A risk examination that is well researched, balanced, and credible will make the proposed program more convincing to higher-level decision makers.

Once the program is under way, it is essential to update the risk assessment frequently. A year-old assessment should not dictate the direction of the program. The threat environment is fluid, changing gradually or sometimes suddenly in response to many factors. Periodic reassessment helps the EP manager ensure that the protective operation is responsive to the risk. The traditional idea of relegating the "security guys" to a basement closet, only to be brought out in an emergency, can be aggressively countered with a credible risk analysis that demonstrates the importance of their immediate presence.

Over time, it is worthwhile to establish a well-informed protective intelligence network. It is hard for the EP manager to develop a protection plan if he or she does not know about the latest threats. One of the most useful sources of protective intelligence is liaison with local, state, and federal law enforcement agencies. The EP manager should seek them out, talk with their chiefs, and cultivate social and business contacts with them. It is easy if the EP manager has a law enforcement background, but even without one, the EP manager should make those contacts anyway. The return on this particular investment can be very profitable.

Program Development

The next step is to write a mission statement that describes the program's goals and objectives. The EP manager should develop that statement through dialogue with decision makers in the organization: the chief of staff, corporate counsel, budget director, and other key members of the chain of command who will review and approve aspects of the program over time.

Budget

It is important to recognize, from the beginning, that one's enthusiasm for a concept or a capital budget item may not necessarily translate into reality. Compromise is usually the foundation of success. The motivation that drives corporations is profit, so it makes sense to learn the company's budget process. If an emergency or unforeseen circumstance requires the EP manager to ask for a budget variance, he or she should be prepared to justify it thoroughly—and also to have alternatives in mind. It is also wise to develop a deep understanding of the company's existing resources, the means for accessing them, and corporate dynamics generally. An EP manager may land in an embarrassing position if he or she seeks approval for an acquisition only to be told that the resource already exists within the corporation or can be acquired more effectively through another route.

Small budget matters deserve careful attention, too. For example, the EP manager should carefully evaluate travel and expense reports from EP staff. It is important to follow corporate expense policies and procedures to the letter. This is particularly relevant if the EP program is new, as it will be the subject of close scrutiny.

Program Design

Whatever benefits decentralization may have in some aspects of business, it can create problems in executive protection. If elements of a company's EP effort are dispersed among many departments (for example, travel planning, storage of threatening letters, and public relations), the EP program may never learn of important developments, plans, and concerns. In such a case, it becomes difficult to collect information, share information, conduct security planning, and ensure completeness of protection. For example, at one multinational corporation, consultants recommended that the EP program collect detailed biographical information about each principal for use in an emergency. EP staff and the principals said it sounded like a good idea. Later, it turned out that such information had already been gathered by the corporate risk management department. Unfortunately, those who would be most likely to respond to an attack against the principals were not aware of that.

If a company's EP elements (intelligence gathering, threat tracking, physical security, training, etc.) are provided by too many different departments and employees and delivered through numerous channels, the result may be disjointed protection. *Disjointed protection leads to gaps, and gaps are what adversaries exploit.* Lack of a central, consistent, and seamless protection strategy makes it easy for key protective elements to be overlooked—and for the protectees to be unclear who they should turn to for help.

Thus, ideally, an EP program should be run by an EP manager, whose duties include proactively searching out threat information; performing, assigning, or contracting for travel advances; arranging locally based, on-site protection services for destinations outside the country; working with the principals' families; and numerous other duties. The position of EP manager should be a high-level position with the authority to centralize the EP operation.

That is true of companies with centralized security functions and those with decentralized security functions. In a large corporation, EP is not necessarily identical with corporate security. Regardless of how security overall may be organized, executive protection is a cross-cutting concern that benefits from having a central, responsible manager. However, that manager can also serve as an on-the-ground EP specialist.

The design and staffing of a corporate EP program also depends on the type of protection needed. If the program will protect the principal solely at the office and the residence, staffing may consist primarily of security officers. By contrast, if the program will also protect the principal when he or she gives speeches to hostile audiences and during travel to dangerous destinations, genuine EP specialists are needed. The number of staff members certainly depends on whether the program is geared toward the work day only or aims to provide protection 24 hours a day, seven days a week.

One other crucial matter in program design is flexibility. Because threat levels can shift suddenly in response to a variety of factors, it does not work to have just barely enough staff providing just barely enough protection. The EP manager should develop and be ready to implement a specific, written plan to ratchet security measures upward if the threat level rises significantly. For example, if credible threats are received, the terrorist threat level jumps, or other warning signs appear, the company may need to temporarily provide round-the-clock personal protection to its principals, provide security drivers at all times, or take other high-security measures. If the threat level jumps up, it is vital to engage in "target hardening" to discourage potential adversaries from taking action. In such situations, it is better to err on the side of caution until the risk appears to subside. Only if the EP manager has built extra capacity into the program—using both in-house and contract staff and other resources—will it be possible to ramp up security measures on short notice.

Personnel Selection

The selection of EP personnel is a potential minefield. Before hiring EP specialists, it is prudent to conduct thorough background investigations, including discussions with current and former associates and employers. It may also be helpful to administer a psychological screening instrument (typically a multiple-choice exam) to help weed out undesirable candidates, if company policy allows such testing. Because the EP staff will spend much time with the protectee (such as the chief executive officer), it pays to find out what personality traits the protectee likes and then use that knowledge, in combination with such criteria as talent and experience, to make personnel selections.

If the corporation has a large security staff, it is worthwhile to consider hiring from within. Doing so represents smart resource management, rewarding good employees who have stayed with the company and creating a visible career ladder that may help minimize turnover among the security staff.

If the EP manager does not hire from within, he or she may need to rely on networking and other creative approaches. In the

EP field, advertising is not the first choice among recruiting methods because an advertisement may divulge the existence of a principal's protection program, whereas a greater level of secrecy may present tactical advantages.

Personnel costs can amount to 85 percent of an EP program's budget. One way to minimize that expense is to use contract protection specialists when appropriate. The use of established, approved contractors can be very useful, especially at distant domestic sites and overseas locations. Contract EP specialists from the destination site will know the language, the customs, and the local players, and the EP program pays them only when needed.

Of course, if the use of contractors is not a viable solution in a given situation, then the EP program should spend whatever is necessary. There is no benefit to skimping on advance work. Any protection professional worth his or her salt knows the value of site preparation in terms of both safety and facilitation. The value of safety is obvious, and facilitation is worth its weight in gold because, at the same time as it increases the principal's comfort and convenience, it also adds immeasurably to the security mission by minimizing unnecessary exposure to risk.

A good practice when the budget is tight, and even when it is not, is for the EP manager to "work the street" on occasion, keeping in touch with the reality of EP operations. Doing so shows the EP staff that the EP manager is proficient in executive protection. It shows the principal that the EP manager is not afraid to get his or her hands dirty and is able to provide operational leadership in addition to administrative leadership.

Training

As was noted in Chapter 6: It's Not About the Gun, reliance on firearms is sometimes overdone. Although an EP program may choose to equip its specialists with guns, it is vital not to depend on them. The alternative, keeping the principal out of harm instead of shooting back at sources of harm, requires extensive training. Training keeps EP staff proficient, interested, and alert—in other words, "switched on." If the program's EP specialists drive the principal, they should take security-oriented driver training. If they carry firearms, they should qualify frequently. If they carry "step-down" weapons (also known as less-lethal weapons, such as TASERs, pepper spray, and various batons), they should receive training in how to use them. Training in emergency medical response—such as the use of cardiopulmonary resuscitation, automated external defibrillators, and advanced first aid equipment—is essential for all EP specialists. For many principals, the likelihood of a non-deliberate emergency (such as a sudden, acute medical problem or a building fire) is greater than the likelihood of a deliberate attack by an adversary.

EP specialists also need training in how to relate to the principal. In executive protection it is a particular challenge to maintain the right relationship with the principal. In an ongoing personal protection situation, an EP specialist may spend a great deal of time close to the principal. However, that does not mean the two are bosom buddies. The EP manager should make sure that EP staff do not develop a relationship with the principal that will affect the protective mission. EP specialists who grow accustomed to the principal's high-end life style may become overly relaxed and begin to participate in that life style, leading them to feel off-duty and "switched off." For example, if the principal is swimming at the Riviera, that is no time for the EP specialist to dive in, too. There are also cases in which the EP specialist's casual attitude decreases the principal's respect for the necessity of the position. In other words, why does the principal need another member of the party? In fact, the principal does not, and the EP specialist should maintain a proper psychological and social distance. Ensuring that the principal and EP staff maintain the right relationship is a key duty of the EP manager.

The following is a list of the most important subjects in which EP specialists should receive training:

protective philosophy	physical defensive skills
working the principal	step-down weapons
choreography of protection	countersurveillance
protective teamwork	liability issues
site advance preparation	residential and office security
vehicle security	trust and confidentiality
10-minute medicine	etiquette
firearms in the protective environment	counterattack driving and avoidance
cover and evacuation	

Program Supervision

Once the EP program has been established, it is important to keep it running well. Periodically, the EP manager should reevaluate the program's direction and procedures to see if the task of protecting the company's principals can be done better. There is room here for imaginative approaches. For example, conducting countersurveillance activities (described in detail in Chapter 5) can reveal the presence of individuals who are watching the principal. The EP manager can set up a plan for watching for the watchers; after all, he or she is being paid to be smarter than they are. By dismantling comfortable assumptions, that kind of proactive behavior can prevent a variety of hazards. Moreover, countersurveillance need not focus solely on outsiders. There are plenty of examples of attacks coming from within.

If the EP manager senses that he or she needs a fresh perspective, it may be time to seek advice from outside the organization. Soliciting help is a sign of strength, maturity, confidence, and a continuing desire to do the best job possible. An outside view may reveal vulnerabilities that an insider cannot see and offer solutions that an insider would never think of.

One outside view from which most EP managers can profit is that of a security engineer. It is true that an EP manager should remain conversant in the matter of security technology, keeping up by reading trade journals and talking with counterparts in other organizations who face similar problems. Nevertheless, it is nearly impossible for the typical EP manager to become sufficiently expert in security technology that he or she can make all the necessary technology decisions without outside help. For example, if a risk assessment shows that the principal needs a high-end security system both at work and at home, it is not the EP manager's task to design it. It is also unsafe to rely solely on the advice of vendors. Especially for large or complex projects, it is better to contract with a security engineering firm, which can design the needed systems and serve as the EP manager's representative in dealings with security hardware vendors and installers. That is just one example of the benefit of turning to outsiders for help when appropriate.

EP Program Image

It can be challenging for an EP program to flourish in the corporate environment. To begin with, the very nature of its presence is negative. An executive protection program is certainly not a profit center; if it operates 24/7, the corporation may not fully fund it, requiring the principal to contribute personal resources; EP staff serve as a constant, unpleasant reminder of the dangers inherent in today's world; and the principal may feel that the presence of EP specialists is a burdensome intrusion, even perhaps an embarrassment if colleagues of equal stature go about their day unprotected. EP presence is usually welcome only as long as the latest kidnapping headline lingers in the principal's mind. Regardless of the program's effectiveness, a negative view of the program—even if that view is uninformed and plain wrong—can scuttle a protection detail just as surely as gross incompetence.

These are difficult negatives to counteract, but they can be minimized. First, it is necessary to get the right players on one's side and make them believers in the program, the EP specialists, and the EP manager—especially in his or her value and ability as a member of corporate management, not just a narrowly focused protection specialist. Skill in executive protection is an obvious requirement for respect, but it is just as important that he EP manager be perceived as an effective, well-informed, and articulate executive who can represent the principal and the corporation in their best light. An EP manager can gain great benefit from fostering a comfortable dialogue with the corporation's major players, keeping them informed, seeking their advice, and being accessible.

Specifically, the EP manager must be savvy enough to recognize current trends in the company and to flow with them. He or she should gain an accurate understanding of the corporate philosophy and mission, as well as the chemistry of key personnel. An EP program is more likely to be supported if it is seen as supporting the corporation's goals. The EP manager and EP specialists should, as much as possible, be team players, in step with the major direction of the corporation. They should rid themselves of any belief that because they represent security and have access to the principal, they are privileged and do not need to conform to the corporate culture. Such an approach engenders resentment, which can eventually sink the program.

Demonstrated performance is one way to help ensure a positive perception of the EP program. However, it takes time to establish a good track record, and many aspects of executive protection are subtle, misunderstood, and rarely seen by anyone but the principal. Therefore, the benefits of the program must be sold to senior leadership and, if necessary, the company's board of directors.

Long-Term Program Survival

The central tenet of an executive protection program, the one that can truly counteract the argument that it is an expensive, intrusive extravagance, is this: It permits the principal to live safely in and move efficiently through this dangerous would. The lack of an overriding concern for personal safety allows him or her to concentrate fully on the business at hand. That is the program's primary selling point. A secondary point worth trumpeting is that, in almost every case, an executive protection program also increases the security of all employees at corporate headquarters.

Numerous real-life examples can demonstrate the genuine, close-to-home hazards of being a prominent chief executive or the family member of one. The EP manager should be prepared to keep the principal and others to whom the program is accountable informed of attacks against executives with profiles similar to that of the principal. (This book's Introduction and Chapter 4 present examples from the recent past, and the EP manager should take care to track new events as they occur.) It may be useful to develop a consistent presentation format (memos, e-mails, PowerPoint presentations) for keeping key parties informed of such events. It is essential to stay informed and on top of events. The last thing an EP manager wants is to be asked by the principal, "What do you think about that kidnapping that happened last night?" and be unable to respond with anything more than a blank stare.

Another way to promote the long-term survival of an EP program is to expand its focus to include related corporate concerns. For example, EP staff can contribute to the development of a crisis management or business continuity program. Lending security expertise to issues other than executive protection integrates the EP program more fully into the corporate community.

If an EP program is to survive and thrive, the EP manager must envision the domino effect of his or her every decision. The future may be a mystery, but executive protection professionals are paid to pierce the fog of the unknown and take smart steps to reach their goals. Through risk assessment, intelligence gathering, countersurveillance, extensive training, appropriate staff supervision, effective preparation, and wise navigation of corporate waters, EP managers stand the best chance of accomplishing their mission: to protect executives so they can carry out the organization's business safely and without fear.

Appendix

A. Mail Screening Tips

From the document "Mail Bombs," produced by the U.S. Postal Inspection Service. Available at http://www.usps.com/postalinspectors/bombs.htm.

It is important to be alert for suspicious parcels, but keep in mind that a mail bomb is an extremely rare occurrence. To illustrate just how rare, Postal Inspectors have investigated an average of 16 mail bombs over the last few years. By contrast, each year, the Postal Service processed over 170 billion pieces of mail. That means during the last few years, the chances that a piece of mail actually contains a bomb average far less than one in 10 billion!

Still, those who are familiar with the characteristics of suspect parcels can help to avert a tragedy. This actually occurred in 1991, when a Dumfries, VA, letter carrier identified a suspect parcel in a collection box. The parcel contained a bomb intended for the sender's estranged husband. By acting quickly, the carrier may have saved the man's life. Although the appearance of mail bombs may vary greatly, here are some characteristics that have repeatedly shown up:

- Mail bombs may have excessive postage. Normally a bomber does not want to mail a parcel over the counter and have to deal face-to-face with a window clerk.

- The return address may be fictitious or non-existent.

- The postmark may show a different location than the return address.

- Mail bombs may bear restricted endorsements, such as "Personal" or "Private." This is particularly important when the addressee does not usually receive personal mail at the office.

- Mail bombs may display distorted handwriting, or the

name and address may be prepared with homemade labels or cut-and-paste lettering.

- Parcel bombs may be unprofessionally wrapped with several combinations of tape used to secure the package, and may be endorsed "Fragile—Handle With Care" or "Rush—Do Not Delay."

- Letter bombs may feel rigid or appear uneven or lopsided.

- Package bombs may have an irregular shape, soft spots, or bulges.

- Mail bombs may have protruding wires, aluminum foil, or oil stains, and may emit a peculiar odor.

While the overwhelming volume of mail does not permit the Postal Service to screen every piece, Postal Inspectors are able to respond quickly if a suspect article is discovered. Each Inspection Service field division has trained and equipped bomb specialists available to provide professional assistance. If you become suspicious of a mailing and are unable to verify the contents, observe the following safety precautions:

- Don't open the article.

- Isolate the suspect parcel and evacuate the immediate area.

- Don't put it in water or a confined space, such as a desk drawer or cabinet.

- If possible, open windows in the immediate area to assist in venting potentially explosive gases.

- Don't worry about possible embarrassment if the item turns out to be innocent. Instead, contact the Postal Inspection Service and your local police department.

B. Bomb Threat Card

A card like this can be printed on narrow stock and placed under telephones to help employees who receive bomb threats.

Time Call Received: **Date:** **Exact wording of bomb threat:** **Listen--do not interrupt! After caller stops volunteering information, ask these questions, trying to keep the caller on the line:** 1. When is the bomb going to explode? 2. Where is the bomb right now? 3. What does the bomb look like? 4. What kind of bomb is it? 5. What will cause the bomb to explode? 6. Did you place the bomb? 7. Why? 8. What is your address? 9. What is your name? **Record the following information:** Sex of caller: Age: Length of call: Telephone number at which call was received: **Bomb threat language (check the appropriate descriptors):** Well-spoken Foul (educated) Taped Incoherent Threat Read Irrational	**Caller's voice (check the appropriate descriptors):** Calm Disguised Angry Soft Excited Loud Slow Laughter Rapid Crying Distinct Normal Ragged Whispered Cracking Nasal Voice Deep Breathing Accent Stutter Slurred Clearing Throat Deep Lisp Rasp *If familiar, who does it sound like?* **Background sounds (check the appropriate descriptors):** Street Noises Voices Factory Animal Machinery Noises Crockery Clear PA System Static House Noises Local Long Distance Motor Booth Music Office Machinery Other: _____ **Your Remarks:** Your name: Your position: **Report the call immediately to:**

C. Checklists for Advance Work

The following checklists are also available in electronic form at www.rloatman.com/book_downloads. Username: surveys. Password: ep$pecialist.

Executive Protection: Master List of Advance Checklists

Travel Destination: _____
Form completed by: _____
Date completed: _____

Checklists, while no substitute for on-the-ground judgment, are an invaluable tool for capturing details about a site, ensuring that no key steps are overlooked, and preserving information that can be used on future trips.

PRINCIPAL PROFILE
Completed by (name): _____
Date completed: _____
Comments: _____
_____

PRE-ADVANCE
Completed by (name): _____
Date completed: _____
Comments: _____
_____

DESTINATION RISK PROFILE
Completed by (name): _____
Date completed: _____
Comments: _____
_____

DETAIL AND COMMAND POST
Completed by (name): _____
Date completed: _____
Comments: _____
_____

COMMERCIAL AIR TRAVEL
Completed by (name): _____
Date completed: _____
Comments: _____
_____

PRIVATE AIR TRAVEL
Completed by (name): _____
Date completed: _____
Comments: _____
_____

LUGGAGE
Completed by (name): _____
Date completed: _____
Comments: _____

GROUND TRANSPORTATION
Completed by (name): _____
Date completed: _____
Comments: _____
_____

ROUTE
Completed by (name): _____
Date completed: _____
Comments: _____
_____

HOTEL
Completed by (name): _____
Date completed: _____
Comments: _____
_____

RESTAURANT
Completed by (name): _____
Date completed: _____
Comments: _____
_____

EMERGENCY MEDICAL CARE
Completed by (name): _____
Date completed: _____
Comments: _____
_____

NOTES
_____
_____
_____
_____
_____
_____
_____
_____

Executive Protection: Principal Profile

Name of principal: _____
Company name: _____
Position: _____
Company address: _____

_____

Phone: _____
Mobile phone: _____

Administrative assistant. Name: _____
   Phone: _____
   Mobile phone: _____

Spouse. Name: _____
   Mobile phone: _____
Residence address: _____

_____

Residence phone: _____

Secondary home (if applicable). Address: _____

_____

   Phone: _____

Passport. Country: _____
   Number: _____
   Expiration date: _____
Driver's license. State: _____
   Number: _____
   Expiration date: _____

Basic physical description of principal (e.g., height, weight, coloring, eyeglasses, hearing aids): _____

_____

Distinguishing features (birthmarks, etc.): _____

Blood type: _____
Date of birth: _____
Place of birth: _____

Principal's primary doctor. Name: _____
   Phone: _____
Principal's dentist. Name: _____

Phone: _____
Principal's usual pharmacy. Name: _____
   Phone: _____
Special medical needs (e.g., medicine, equipment): _____

_____

Children's names, schools, school principals, school phone:

_____
_____
_____
_____
_____

Have digital photo of principal: □
   Of spouse: □
   Of children: □
Where are the photos? _____
DNA kit completed. □ Kept where? _____
Fingerprints on file. □ Kept where? _____
Handwriting sample on file. □ Kept where? _____
Digital video of principal. □ Kept where? _____
Medical power of attorney for principal. □ Kept where? ____

_____

To be attached:
   Current photo of principal. □
   Photocopy of main passport pages. □

NOTES

_____
_____
_____
_____
_____
_____
_____
_____
_____
_____
_____
_____

Executive Protection: Pre-Advance Checklist

Travel Destination: _____
Form completed by: _____
Date completed: _____

This task does not require travel; it can be done with a telephone and computer. Gather key facts, make initial contacts, and consult files from previous trips to the location. Use judgment: if more or different information is needed, get it and note it at end or attach it.

TRIP BASICS

Date/time EP notified of trip: _____
Point of contact. Position: _____
    Phone _____
Principal. Name: _____
    Title: _____
    Office phone: _____
    Home phone: _____
    Mobile phone: _____
Destination(s): _____
    Departure date: _____
    Return date: _____
Trip coordinator. Name: _____
    Title: _____
    Phone: _____
    Fax: _____
    E-mail: _____
    Other (e.g., pager): _____

EP DETAIL

Number of EP specialists assigned: _____
Positions assigned (circle and write #): supervisor, advance, close-in protection
Using a support detail? _____
If so, circle: contract or in-country security employee
    Name/title: _____
    Phone: _____
    Mobile phone: _____
    Fax: _____
    E-mail: _____

EP specialist #1. Name: _____
    Position: _____
    Phone: _____
    Mobile phone: _____
    Fax: _____
    E-mail: _____

EP specialist #2. Name: _____
    Position: _____
    Phone: _____
    Mobile phone: _____
    Fax: _____
    E-mail: _____

EP specialist #3. Name: _____
    Position: _____
    Phone: _____
    Mobile phone: _____
    Fax: _____
    E-mail: _____

EP specialist #4. Name: _____
    Position: _____
    Phone: _____
    Mobile phone: _____
    Fax: _____
    E-mail: _____

HISTORICAL TRIP REVIEW

Review files for the two most recent trips to this location.
Case file #: _____ Trip date: _____
EP specialist: _____

Case file #: _____ Trip date: _____
EP specialist: _____

TRIP ACTIVITIES

Itinerary attached (circle): yes, no
Purpose of trip: _____
Other members of party. Name: _____
    Title/affiliation: _____
Type of special activity, if any: _____
    Location: _____
    Dates: _____
    Special clothing or gear needed by principal: _____

Executive Protection:
Pre-Advance Checklist

TRANSPORTATION
Air travel

Commercial. Airports: _____

   Airline: _____

   Phone: _____

   Reservation number: _____

   Seat number/type: _____

Obtained map of airport terminal (circle): yes, no

Identify key locations (circle): terminal that principal will likely use, airline club lounges, baggage claim area, VIP services location and phone number, pickup and drop-off areas, parking areas, airport police.

Contact information for list above: _____

_____

_____

Private. Airport: _____

   Aircraft call sign/tail number: _____

   Chief pilot. Name: _____

   Mobile phone: _____

   FBO: _____

   Contact name/title/phone: _____

_____

   FBO hours and services: _____

_____

   Need ramp steps (circle)? yes, no

   Hangar available (circle)? yes, no

Helicopter. Heliport: _____

   Tail number: _____

Chief pilot. Name: _____

   Mobile phone: _____

Heliport hours and services: _____

_____

Ground transportation

Vendor: _____

Address: _____

Phone: _____

Mobile phone: _____

E-mail: _____

Obtained route maps (circle): yes, no

Number and type of vehicles: _____

_____

Vehicle that principal will ride in. Year/make/model: _____

License number: _____

   Seat configuration: _____

Driver. Name: _____

   Phone: _____

   Mobile phone: _____

Have photograph (circle)? yes, no

Background completed (circle)? yes, no

Support vehicle(s). Year/make/model: _____

   License number: _____

   Seat configuration: _____

Driver. Name: _____

   Phone: _____

   Mobile phone: _____

Have photograph (circle)? yes, no

Background completed (circle)? yes, no

Other transportation (water, rail). Provide details: _____

_____

_____

International travel concerns

Note key facts on:

   Customs: _____

   Immigration/visas (work versus personal): _____

_____

   Vaccinations: _____

   Language/interpreters: _____

   U.S. embassy or consulate contact info: _____

_____

NEARBY MEDICAL CARE

Hospital. Address: _____

   Phone: _____

Ambulance co. Address: _____

   Phone: _____

Private doctor. Name: _____

   Address: _____

   Phone: _____

Medical evacuation. Co. name: _____

   Contact name: _____

   Phone: _____

Executive Protection:
Pre-Advance Checklist

LOCAL HOST OR SPONSOR
Name/title: _____
Organization: _____
Phone: _____

EXPECTED LOCAL CONDITIONS DURING VISIT
Crime concerns: _____
Political or social turmoil (circle): strikes; riots; malice toward principal, company, or people fitting principal's profile
  Details: _____
Holidays during trip. Names/dates: _____
Weather: _____

LODGING FOR PRINCIPAL
Hotel: _____
  Address: _____
  Phone: _____
  Reservation/billing under what name: _____
  Type of room/suite: _____
  Confirmation no.: _____
General manager. Name: _____
  Phone: _____
  Mobile phone: _____
Security director. Name: _____
  Phone: _____
  Mobile phone: _____
Concierge phone: _____
Head of housekeeping. Name: _____
  Phone: _____
Character of hotel's neighborhood: _____
Food service options/hours: _____

If not hotel, will principal lodge at (circle one): principal's secondary residence, other private residence, private yacht, other location?
Owner/host: _____
Address: _____
Contact person: _____
Phone: _____

LODGING FOR EP STAFF
Same as for principal (circle): yes, no
If not: Hotel: _____
  Address: _____
  Phone: _____
  Reservation/billing under what name: _____

Number of rooms: _____
  Confirmation no.: _____

LOCAL LAW ENFORCEMENT CONTACTS
Agency name: _____
Contact person: _____
Phone: _____
Address: _____
Likely response time: _____

PRIVATE SECURITY CONTACTS
Organization: _____
Contact person: _____
Phone: _____
Mobile phone: _____
Capabilities if needed: _____
_____

NOTES
_____
_____
_____
_____
_____
_____
_____
_____
_____
_____
_____
_____
_____
_____
_____
_____
_____
_____
_____
_____
_____
_____
_____
_____
_____
_____
_____
_____

230

Executive Protection:
Destination Risk Profile

Travel Destination: _____
Form completed by: _____
Date completed: _____

Though most of the items below apply to both domestic and international travel, a few apply only to international travel.

SOURCES TO CONSULT
- ☐ EP specialists who have been to the destination
- ☐ Checklists, reports, and notes from previous trips to the destination
- ☐ Overseas Security Advisory Council (OSAC)
- ☐ U.S. State Department Travel Advisories
- ☐ World Wide Web, including news reports about the destination
- ☐ Commercial travel intelligence provider (e.g., iJET)
- ☐ Intelligence sources at the destination (e.g., security, law enforcement, or business contacts)—ask about security considerations you may not have thought of
- ☐ Regional security officer (RSO) at U.S. embassy or consulate at destination (ask specifically about crime concerns, local law enforcement, local security providers, car services, interpreters, and any laws or customs that an EP operation should know about)
- ☐ Principal's threat file

CHARACTERISTICS OF TRIP
Purpose of trip (business, pleasure, meeting with controversial people or organizations): _____

Main activities of trip: _____

Unusual, potentially risky activities on trip: _____

FINDINGS BY CATEGORY
Crime conditions: _____
_____
_____

Other challenging conditions (demonstrations, strikes, riots, holidays): _____
_____
_____

Expected exposure to possible threats (much local travel, meetings with hostile audiences, open-admission speeches, other public appearances): _____
_____

Proximity, speed, and quality of emergency response.
Police: _____
_____

Fire: _____
_____

Emergency medical response: _____
_____

Possibility of medical evacuation: _____
_____

Hostile attitudes toward company, principal, or people who share principal's profile (e.g., U.S. businesspeople, wealthy persons, women in business): _____
_____
_____ \

Possibility that EP specialists can carry concealed firearms if deemed necessary: _____
_____

Risks related to any special events the principal will participate in: _____
_____

Other relevant findings: _____
_____
_____

PRELIMINARY RISK RATING
Initial estimate of risk level for principal at this destination (circle): high, medium, low

NOTES
_____
_____
_____
_____
_____
_____
_____
_____
_____

Executive Protection: Detail and Command Post

EP supervisor/manager. Name: _____
  Mobile phone: _____
Historical data reviewed to determine staffing levels? yes/no
Advance EP specialist. Name: _____
  Mobile phone: _____
EP specialist 1. Name: _____
  Mobile phone: _____
EP specialist 2. Name: _____
  Mobile phone: _____
EP specialist 3. Name: _____
  Mobile phone: _____

Will EP staff be armed? yes, no, some
  Carry permits confirmed? yes, no
For each position, check corporate employee or contractor:

	Corporate Employee	Contractor
EP supervisor		
Advance agent 1		
EP specialist 1 (EP1)		
EP specialist 2 (EP2)		
EP specialist 3 (EP3)		
Driver for principal		
Driver for other vehicle		
Command post officer		
Other staff		

Collect required information about any security or other contractors retained. For example:
  Name: _____
  Organization: _____
  Address: _____
  Phone: _____
  Mobile phone: _____
  Law enforcement officer? yes, no
  If so, permission to work part-time? yes/no
  If civilian, licensed to work security in the jurisdiction? yes/no
  Licensed to carry concealed firearm? yes/no
  Daily pay rate: _____
  Per diem: _____
  References: _____
  Other: _____

Has EP supervisor inspected all personnel, including contractors, for compliance? yes/no
Dress code for detail: _____
Has EP supervisor provided EP team with security briefing based on risk assessment? yes/no
Command post location: _____
  Hours of operation: _____
  If technical surveillance countermeasures are required, who will perform service? _____
Determine what technology or other resources the detail will need for the following purposes. Ensure availability.
  Communication: _____
  Navigation: _____
  Tracking: _____
  Photography: _____
  Information gathering: _____
  Alarm systems: _____
  Emergency response: _____
If establishing on-site command post, decide which items it will need and then arrange to obtain them:

- ☐ suitable room with tables and chairs
- ☐ chalk board or bulletin board
- ☐ local phone book
- ☐ spare batteries
- ☐ flashlights
- ☐ portable alarms
- ☐ surveillance equipment
- ☐ city and neighborhood maps
- ☐ fire escape route map
- ☐ radios and chargers
- ☐ office supplies
- ☐ fire extinguisher
- ☐ panic alarms for principals
- ☐ portable alarms
- ☐ diagrams of hotel, meeting locations, etc.
- ☐ advanced first aid supplies and equipment
- ☐ long phone cord
- ☐ notebook computers with Internet access
- ☐ food services

Track the equipment that EP specialists take for the assignment (e.g., radio, firearm, camera, surveillance equipment). Remind them of their responsibility for the equipment.

	Equipment Types and Serial #s	Date Taken	Date Returned
EP1			
EP2			
EP3			

Executive Protection:
Commercial Air Travel

City: _____
Form completed by: _____
Date completed: _____

Departure airport. Name: _____
  Address: _____
  Web address: _____
  Checked Web site for useful information? yes/no

Airline/flight number: _____
  Class/seat number: _____
Airline phone. Reservations: _____
  Customer service: _____

Airport security director. Name: _____
  Phone: _____
  Mobile phone: _____
  Notified that a VIP is coming: yes/no Date: _____

Airport police: _____
  Phone: _____

Airport VIP services. Name: _____
  Phone: _____

Airport hours of operation: _____

Obtained map of airport/terminals/parking: yes, no

Best drop-off location: _____
_____

Need/have passport? _____

Have tip money for baggage handlers? yes/no

Luggage check-in location identified/any special arrangements made: _____

Principal's carry-on luggage free of prohibited items? yes/no

Boarding pass machines available? yes/no

Airline club location: _____

Restroom locations: _____

Security checkpoint waiting time estimate from www.tsa.gov:
_____

Customs/immigration facilitation arrangements made, if applicable? _____

Medical assistance available on-site? _____

Other amenities at airport:
- business center
- baggage assistance
- newsstand/bookstore
- convenience store
- gift shop
- ATM
- currency exchange
- shoe shine
- restaurants (sit down, carry out)

Is airport under TSA "notice of deficient security" (check www.tsa.gov)? yes/no

Advance checklist completed for destination airport? yes/no

NOTES

_____
_____
_____
_____
_____
_____
_____
_____
_____
_____
_____
_____
_____
_____
_____
_____
_____
_____

233

Executive Protection:
Private Air Travel

City: _____
Form completed by: _____
Date completed: _____

Departure date/time: _____
Airport. Name: _____
   Address: _____
   Phone: _____
   Web address: _____
   Checked Web site for useful information? yes/no
Airport security contact: _____
   Phone: _____
   Mobile phone: _____
Airport police: _____
   Phone: _____

FBO (e.g., Signature, Million Air). Name: _____
   Address: _____
   Contact person: _____
   Hours of operation: _____

Police jurisdiction (department name): _____

_____
   Phone: _____
Nearby ambulance service. Name: _____
   Phone: _____
   Response time: _____
Nearest hospital with trauma unit. Name: _____
   Address: _____

   Phone: _____

Have map of airport layout (entrance, parking)? yes, no
Does airport/FBO perimeter security appear adequate? yes/no
Does FBO access control appear adequate? yes/no
Secure waiting area available? yes/no
Need/have passport? _____
Principal's carry-on luggage free of prohibited items? yes/no
Best drop-off location: _____

_____
Allowed to drive onto ramp? yes/no

Aircraft. Year/make: _____
   Tail number: _____
   Hours of flight time: _____
   Fuel range: _____

Passenger capacity: _____
Luggage capacity: _____
Interior layout and facilities: _____

_____
Number of flight attendants on aircraft, if any: _____
Chief pilot. Name: _____
   Mobile phone: _____
Copilot. Name: _____
   Mobile phone: _____

Principal's medical information available? yes/no
Catering arranged? yes/no   Date: _____
Services available:
   ☐ mechanics
   ☐ fuel
   ☐ de-icing equipment

EP staff transporting firearms? yes/no. If so, type of arrangement made: _____

Expected arrival time at destination airport: _____
Destination airport. Name: _____
   Address: _____
   Phone: _____
   Hours of operation: _____
   Runway length: _____
   Restrictions on night landings, noise, and type of aircraft:

_____
Alternative arrival FBOs in case of bad weather or emergency.
   1. Name: _____
   Address: _____
   Phone: _____
   Distance from primary arrival FBO: _____
   2. Name: _____
   Address: _____
   Phone: _____
   Distance from primary arrival FBO: _____
Ground transportation options from those sites: _____

_____
Advance checklist completed for destination airport? yes/no

Executive Protection: Luggage

Travel Destination:	_____
Form completed by:	_____
Date completed:	_____

ALL TRAVEL

- ☐ Place color-coded tags—without any names—on all the luggage. For example, use blue for principal and red for second executive. Change the colors periodically.

- ☐ After flight, remove name tags from luggage but keep color tags on. Then, at hotel, the EP specialist can say to the bellman, "Take the bags with red tags to room 320 and the bags with blue tags to room 322." That way, it is not necessary to mention the principal's name in the lobby or at the curb.

- ☐ Ensure that principal's carry-on luggage contains no prohibited items. Double-check carry-on list at www.tsa.gov.

- ☐ Ensure that principal's checked luggage contains no prohibited items. Double-check packing list at www.tsa.gov.

- ☐ Pack EP staff contact information inside the luggage in case a bag gets lost.

COMMERCIAL AIR TRAVEL

- ☐ Encourage light packing. Fewer bags = less time waiting in crowded luggage carousel area.

- ☐ Checked luggage may be searched, so remind principal not to put sensitive business papers there.

- ☐ Checked luggage may be x-rayed, so remind principal not to place camera film there.

- ☐ Leave checked bags unlocked so TSA can search without breaking locks. Alternative: use "TSA accepted and recognized locks" or luggage with those locks built in. TSA screeners can unlock and relock such equipment during a search.

- ☐ Use luggage tags without principal's name. Use company name or EP specialist's name. Use business, not home, address.

- ☐ Watch for colored luggage tag to speed EP team's identification, collection, and transport of the luggage.

- ☐ Maintain close custody of luggage to be checked and also of carry-on items (to prevent others from placing dangerous or illegal items into principal's or EP specialist's bags).

PRIVATE AIR TRAVEL

- ☐ Use color-coding luggage tag system to ensure that only the correct luggage is placed aboard the aircraft.

- ☐ Do not allow unknown packages or luggage to be introduced onto the aircraft.

- ☐ If risk level warrants it, screen luggage with small X ray machine.

Complete the following table:

Traveler	Luggage Tag Color Code	Number of Pieces
Principal and family		
Guest 1		
Guest 2		
EP1		
EP2		
Chief pilot		
Copilot		
Other		
Other		

NOTES

_____
_____
_____
_____
_____
_____
_____
_____
_____
_____
_____
_____
_____
_____
_____

Executive Protection: Ground Transportation

City: _____
Form completed by: _____
Date completed: _____

VEHICLES

Number of vehicles required: _____

Number of vehicles from each source:

Car rental agency: _____
  Phone: _____
  Reservation # _____ :
Car service: _____
  Phone: _____
  Reservation #: _____
Contracted EP car service: _____
  Phone: _____
  Reservation #: _____
Principal's personal car: _____
Corporate car: _____

Using protected (armored) vehicle to transport principal? yes/no

Complete the following table:

	Make	Model	Color	License #
Vehicle 1				
Vehicle 2				
Vehicle 3				

Secure parking arranged? yes/no. If so, where: _____

  If not, will car be watched by security staff? yes/no

Will detail use a lead car? yes/no Follow car? yes/no

Preferred seating arrangement (for principal, guests, and EP staff): _____

Vehicle maintenance up-to-date? yes/no
Gas tanks full? yes/no
Vehicle clean, inside and out? yes/no
Vehicle security check conducted? yes/no
  By whom/date: _____

EQUIPMENT

Check the box if item is needed and available. Draw a line through item if not applicable.

- ☐ bomb mirror
- ☐ spare tire & jack
- ☐ flashlights
- ☐ flares or reflectors
- ☐ umbrella
- ☐ basic tools
- ☐ GPS
- ☐ cash or credit card for fuel
- ☐ fire extinguisher
- ☐ spare keys
- ☐ jumper cables
- ☐ advanced first aid kit
- ☐ automated external defibrillator
- ☐ maps
- ☐ registration and proof of insurance
- ☐ toll pass to speed passage through tool booths

DRIVERS

Has EP supervisor briefed drivers on:

- ☐ Threats, e.g., kidnap attempt, being run off road, carjacking, assassination attempt
- ☐ Security measures, e.g., keeping doors locked, not leaving car unattended, keeping motor running as principal enters and exits the vehicle
- ☐ Courtesies, e.g., expected dress, demeanor, use of radio, keeping mobile phone on but set to vibrate

Do drivers have cash to tip valets so cars can be kept close to entrance of hotel, office building, conference center, etc.? yes/no

Complete the following table:

Driver Name	Has Valid License	Mobile Phone #

Background screening conducted on all contract drivers? yes/no

Executive Protection: Route Survey

City: _____
Form completed by: _____
Date completed: _____

Date of movement: _____
Scheduled departure time: _____

Starting address: _____
_____

Destination address: _____
_____

Contact person at destination. Name: _____
   Phone: _____

Distance: _____
Expected duration of drive: _____

Principal being transported (name): _____
Number in principal's party: _____

Number of vehicles to be used: _____

In designing routes, minimize chokepoints and maximize speed and safe havens.

Primary route: _____
_____
_____
_____

Secondary route: _____
_____
_____
_____

Tertiary route: _____
_____
_____
_____

Has a member of the EP team driven the route at the same time and day of week as the planned trip?

Note: If this is a recurring run, vary the route if possible.

Check on the following changeable conditions:

□ possible traffic problems or road closures due to special events, such as parades, demonstrations, sporting events, or rock concerts (check with law enforcement contacts or local government officials). Notes: _____
_____

□ existing traffic problems (listen to radio station traffic reports and check on-line traffic sources). Notes: _____
_____

□ construction zones, drawbridges, railroad crossing, toll plazas. Notes: _____
_____

□ weather-related road problems (snow, flooding, high winds that affect bridge traffic). Notes: _____
_____

Note any unavoidable risk locations along the route:
□ bridges
□ overpasses
□ railroad tracks
□ school zones

Identify safe havens along the route:
□ hospitals: _____
_____

□ police stations: _____
_____

□ firehouses: _____
_____

Will countersurveillance team be used in other vehicles?
yes/no

NOTES
_____
_____
_____
_____
_____
_____
_____
_____
_____

Executive Protection:
Hotel Survey

Travel Destination: _____
Form completed by: _____
Date completed: _____

If possible, conduct advance at same time of day principal will arrive. That is the best way to see what the conditions will be like when the principal comes and to meet the staff who will be on duty then.

Hotel. Name: _____
    Address: _____
    _____
    Phone: _____
    Web address: _____
    Checked Web site for useful information? yes/no
General manager. Name: _____
    Phone: _____
Security manager. Name: _____
    Phone: _____
    Security resources that may help EP detail: _____
    _____

Principal's expected arrival date/time: _____
Principal's expected departure date/time: _____
Type of lodging for principal (e.g., room on executive level, suite, etc.): _____
Requested location of room (e.g., high, low, away from elevators, etc.): _____
Room #: _____
Room phone number: _____
Reservation #: _____
Reservation under what name? _____

Concierge. Name: _____
    Phone: _____
Bell captain. Name: _____
    Phone: _____
Housekeeping manager. Name: _____
    Phone: _____
Food service manager. Name: _____
    Phone: _____
Valet parking manager. Name: _____
    Phone: _____
    Arrangements made to keep EP team's vehicle(s) near entrance? yes, no

Obtained map of hotel? yes, no
EP familiar with hotel layout? yes, no

Best entrances and exits for principal: _____
_____
Alternate entrances and exits: _____

Emergency exits/stairwells. Direction from principal's room:
_____
# of doors from principal's room to fire stairwell: _____
# of doors from EP staff's room to principal's room: _____
Is there reason to believe the hotel's fire detection and suppression systems are not adequate? yes, no
Location of fire extinguishers: _____

Has check-in been arranged so that the principal can walk directly to room and bypass the front desk? yes, no
Will the principal's mobile phone work throughout the hotel? yes, no
Will the EP staff's mobile phones work throughout the hotel? yes, no

What amenities are available on-site?
- ☐ broadband Internet
- ☐ massage
- ☐ pool
- ☐ barber/beautician
- ☐ laundry and dry cleaning
- ☐ retail stores
- ☐ exercise room
- ☐ business center
- ☐ restaurants
- ☐ room service dining
- ☐ other: _____

Responding police department. Name: _____
    Phone: _____
Responding fire department. Name: _____
    Phone: _____
Closest ambulance service. Name: _____
    Phone: _____
Closest hospital with trauma center. Name: _____
    Phone: _____
    Distance/time from hotel: _____

Attach to this form:
- ☐ hotel brochure
- ☐ hotel floor plan
- ☐ emergency evacuation
- ☐ medevac procedure

Executive Protection:
Restaurant Survey

Restaurant. Name:_____
  Address:_____
_____
  Phone: _____
  Cuisine (e.g., French, Italian): _____
  Web address: _____
  Checked Web site for useful information? yes/no

Manager's name: _____
  Contacted about special requirements? yes, no
Maitre d's name: _____
  Contacted about special requirements? yes, no

Vehicle considerations. Where can principal's vehicle be
kept? _____
  Valet parking available? _____

Best entrance for principal: _____

Location of exits: _____
_____

Restrooms. Location: _____
  Safe and suitable? _____

Dress code: _____

Manager informed of seating requirements for principal and
EP specialists (e.g., private room, away from front window)?
yes, no

Reservations. For what time? _____
  Under what name? _____
  Size of party? _____
  When booked and by whom? _____

Is there reason to believe the restaurant's fire detection and
suppression systems are not adequate? yes, no

Will the principal's mobile phone work inside the restaurant?
yes, no

Will the EP staff's mobile phones work inside the restaurant?
yes, no

Other suitable restaurants nearby (in case of a problem with
primary restaurant):

  Name: _____
  Address: _____
  Cuisine: _____

  Name: _____
  Address: _____
  Cuisine: _____

Responding police department. Name: _____
  Phone: _____

Responding fire department. Name: _____
  Phone: _____

Closest ambulance service. Name: _____
  Phone: _____

Closest hospital with trauma center. Name: _____
  Phone: _____
  Distance/time from hotel: _____

NOTES:
_____
_____
_____
_____
_____
_____
_____
_____
_____
_____
_____
_____
_____

Copyright © 2006 R. L. Oatman & Associates, Inc.

Executive Protection:
Emergency Medical Care

City: _____
Form completed by: _____
Date completed: _____

HOSPITAL

Name: _____

Address: _____

_____

Phone: _____

Web address: _____

Checked Web site for useful information? yes/no

Emergency room contact. Name: _____

    Phone: _____

Is facility advanced enough to stabilize any injury or medical condition? yes, no

If not, what level of medical emergency would require evacuation to another hospital? _____

_____

Helicopter and pad available? yes, no

If outside home country, is principal eligible to use this hospital? yes, no

Does hospital have a suitable blood supply (especially relevant for foreign travel)? yes, no

English-speaking doctors or interpreters? yes, no

Arrangements made for emergency medical evacuation to home country or city? yes, no

Is principal's insurance accepted at hospital? yes, no

What types of specialists can hospital call on? _____

_____

How quickly can they reach hospital? _____

Location of emergency room entrance: _____

_____

Location of nearest 24-hour pharmacy? _____

_____

Is the principal's choice of clergy available if needed? yes, no

Will hospital allow EP specialist to remain with the principal at all times? yes, no

DOCTOR'S OFFICE

In case the principal needs to see a doctor but does not need to visit a hospital emergency room, list nearby offices of recommended doctors.

General practitioner. Name: _____

    Address: _____

    _____

    Phone: _____

Other specialty that principal might need (based on his or her medical history): _____

    Specialist's name: _____

    Address: _____

    _____

    Phone: _____

Another specialty that principal might need (based on his or her medical history): _____

    Specialist's name: _____

    Address: _____

    _____

    Phone: _____

AMBULANCE

Closest ambulance service. Name: _____

    Phone: _____

    Estimated response time: _____

NOTES:

_____
_____
_____
_____
_____
_____
_____
_____
_____
_____

Index

9/11, EP significance of, 10
access control, 18
advance
  airport, 139
  checklists, 132, 143
  ground transportation, 140
  lodging, 142
  pre-advance, 135
  route, 141
  travel, 20, 131, 166
adversaries
  identifying, 47
AED. *See* automated external
  defibrillator
air travel
  commercial, 139, 170, 172
  private, 19, 171, 177, 181
al Qaeda, 169
alarm systems, 127
Animal Liberation Front, 22
antisurveillance, 84, 93
Armed Security Officer
  Program (TSA), 189
armored car. *See* vehicle,
  protected
armoring levels, 158

Art of Executive Protection, The, 1,
  131
ASIS International, 27, 29, 51,
  195, 199, 201
assassination, 31, 103
asset optimization, 14
asset protection, 12
attack on principal, 103
automated external defibrillator,
  21, 48, 127
baggage. *See* luggage
bomb threats. *See* threats, bomb
bombs, 58, 59, 60, 61, 62
BSR, 199
budget, 208
car service. *See* driver, chauffeur
  or car service
carjacking, 147
case studies, 17, 35, 45, 60, 74
certifications
  EP, 201
  general secuity, 201
Certified Protection
  Professional (CPP), 201, 202
closed-circuit television, 18, 48,
  127

communication center, 165
controversial profile, 21, 39
countersurveillance, 83, 84, 88
crime statistics, 49, 51
Crossroads Training Academy, 199
death of principal, 13
defense contractors, 26
DNA kit, 128
driver
    chauffeur or car service, 21, 150, 151, 164
    EP specialist, 152
    principal, 149
    security, 152
driving
    risks, 145, 147, 149
    security, 20, 21, 77
    training, 160, 164, 199
Earth Liberation Front, 22
e-mail, 117
emergency information packet, 79, 128, 136
encryption, 118
engineer, security, 20
EP program development, 208, 209
EP specialists
    contract, 111, 134
EP, practical value of, 11
evacuation, 8
Exceptional Case Study Project, 30
Federal Air Marshal Service, 173
fire, 170
firearm
    attack with, 66
    defense with, 101, 102, 103
    detection, 109
    permits, 104, 111
    training, 103, 108
flight, not fight, 17
garage solutions, 18
general aviation. See air travel, private
global positioning system (GPS), 118, 119, 129
ground transportation. See driving, security
gun. See firearm
high-stress work environment, 17
home security, 19, 48
hotels, 61, 170
iJET, 125
information exposure
    corporate, 38
    individual, 40
information sources, 43
insider threat, 81
Internet research, 121, 122
Kaczynski, Theodore, 62
kidnap and ransom insurance, 78
kidnapping, 3, 19, 53, 70, 72, 74
Lampert, Edward, 3
Latin America, 53, 71, 151, 169
Law Enforcement Officers' Safety Act, 105
leadership, 205
less-lethal weapons. See step-down weapons
lodging. See hotels
luggage, 140, 175
mail screening, 21, 65
managing an EP detail, 205, 214
mapping. See navigation
medical power of attorney, 137
Mexico, 71
Mexico City, 71, 132
National Highway Traffic Safety Administration, 146
navigation, 119
Oatman School of Executive Protection, 195
office security, 48, 69
OnStar, 118
OPSEC, 94
Overseas Security Advisory Council (OSAC), 122
personnel selection, 211
pharmacy, 44, 80, 137

photography, 120
Physical Security Professional
 (PSP), 202, 203
principal's concerns, 52
proactive approach to EP, 16
Professional Certified
 Investigator (PCI), 202, 203
profile. *See* information exposure
protected vehicle, 77
Red Army Fraction, 8
regional security officer, 138
relationship building, 163, 190
reputation, company, 15
return on investment, 15
risk assessment, 18, 25, 28, 29,
 37, 121, 207
 definition of, 27
risks, range of, 55
route planning, 122, 141, 153
safe havens, 141
safe room, 13, 20, 21
satellite radio, 122
Scotti, Tony, 199
Secret Service, U.S., 30
Security Management magazine, 27
step-down weapons, 112
surveillance, target, 4, 32, 84, 85
systemic approach to EP, 16
tabletop exercises, 78, 188
technology, 115
telephones, mobile, 117, 129

terrorism, 7, 50
 domestic, 22
threat assessment, definition of,
 27
threats
 bomb, 35
 making, 31, 35
 tracking, 22, 34, 66
tracking of principal, 119
training
 driving, 199
 EP, 193, 212
 schools, 194, 195
travel
 dangerous locations, 19, 167,
  169
 planning, 123, 125, 131, 133,
  138, 161, 166
 security of, 49, 162
TSCM, 96
Unabomber, 62
United States Postal Service, 65
Vehicle Dynamics Institute, 199
vehicle, protected, 20, 21, 154
visitors of concern, 90
vulnerability assessment,
 definition of, 27
wealthy persons, 4, 17, 19, 45
workplace violence, 47, 53, 66,
 67

244